Mae
x

The sankofa bird on the cover of this book is a symbol
from Ghana, one that I have been drawn to for many years.
Its beak is either carrying or reaching for an egg, its feet face
forward while its head looks back, advising us to remember
the lessons of the past as we journey on into the new world
of the future—a practice I try to honor, and the spirit of *Kin*.

KIN

Caribbean Recipes
for the Modern Kitchen

Marie Mitchell

Photography by Christian Cassiel

W. W. NORTON & COMPANY

Independent Publishers Since 1923

For B, R, E, D & M

The pieces of my heart here, and for the ones in the wind

We connect.

It's a new year and I'm staring out at the Caribbean Sea, feeling closer to the home I hold in my imagination than in a long time. These last two years I've felt lost, detached from myself. Here in Grenada, though, I've been able to find pockets of me that I thought were gone. The vastness of the sea is both terrifying and inviting—but sitting so close to nature, I feel grounded. Beside the road, goats graze on small tufts of grass, and towering fruit trees sway and rustle in the wind. I close my eyes and hear nothing but nature's sounds, and modern life is drowned out through that single moment of tuning in.

Relaxing on this veranda, a temporary home away from home, I look at my legs and think about the weight they have carried in their lifetime. Not only physical weight, but emotional and spiritual weight, too. I sense how these legs came to me from those who walked before me, mostly people I've never known but whose genes I share, and whose smile I may replicate. This sense of connection feels especially relevant here in Grenada, as it's the island where I was married, and where Mum and I would share our last trip together.

You see, I'm obsessed with legacy and the traces of life that we inherit, then leave behind, and I've never felt this obsession more than since losing those closest to me. There have been three seismic shifts in my life, pain and joy entwined, from one extreme to the other: the loss of my hilarious and charismatic brother, then of my sunshine mother; and finally the moment I became a mama myself. Grief has a way of stripping you to your core, laying bare the basics. I am rebuilding my life with a sense of urgency that has come from understanding that time is short.

Food and the culture surrounding it are maybe the purest forms of legacy. Food sustains us, it marks our most precious moments, and it reveals our shared and

7

forgotten histories. The Dutch pots and hidden fire pits that our enslaved ancestors used to cook foraged ingredients or scraps, to make the meals we eat today with pride—they are what make us "us." To some people, jerk or oil down may be mere recipes, but to me they are expressions of resourcefulness and resilience, of celebration and joy.

And what better history to draw upon than that of my own parents, Earle and Barbara? They were both eight when they left the warm, slow pace of life in Jamaica, with yards full of banana, mango, and breadfruit trees to be picked and chickens to be chased, to emigrate to cold, cramped England, where parents and children were expected to share all of life in one room. Food was always a powerful reminder of where they'd come from, and never was there a sweeter moment than watching Mum eat the fruits of her homeland, becoming giddy with excitement, forever young in that place where she didn't get to grow up.

Kin is a love letter to my Caribbean identity, a journey through the region's food that lets me immortalize my love for my family, including all those who walked before me. I started writing the book a few months before I became a parent; a time when I was thinking a lot about past generations. Then, suddenly, I lost my mum, and Marcie was born a few weeks later. *Kin* was always going to be about the joy of being from the Caribbean and the different ways that community—my community— is bound together, but it's now also a tribute to my first family, the Mitchells, a record of a little family from South London who have touched so many lives.

For the first two years of my life, we lived in government- subsidized housing opposite Battersea Park. After that, we moved to Putney, but even once we were there, up until I was a teen, my dad and I would regularly return to that green space as a Sunday ritual. It felt like freedom.

The adventure playground—feelings of invincibility as I scaled new heights—is still etched in my mind. As is the bandstand where my cousins and I played chase, before devouring a begged-for ice cream while walking back to the parking lot.

Saturdays, meanwhile, were spent running errands and picking up weekly supplies with Mum from the Arndale Center, now known as Southside. As we walked down the concourse, the smell of freshly fried doughnuts would fill our nostrils. The 'ethnic' shops would have produce lined up outside, just like you see in London's Brixton, Ridley Road or Walthamstow markets to this day. The goods were secured—hard dough bread, buns, the Sunday staples of plantain, green banana and yam. The hard dough would make it home, minus a few little torn parts

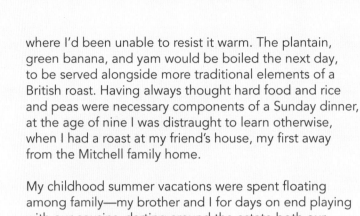

where I'd been unable to resist it warm. The plantain, green banana, and yam would be boiled the next day, to be served alongside more traditional elements of a British roast. Having always thought hard food and rice and peas were necessary components of a Sunday dinner, at the age of nine I was distraught to learn otherwise, when I had a roast at my friend's house, my first away from the Mitchell family home.

My childhood summer vacations were spent floating among family—my brother and I for days on end playing with our cousins, darting around the estate both our parents had grown up in. The playground was small, but it felt like our patch, and we headed back to our auntie's house only when we needed feeding. Our nan lived down the road, and whenever we landed there, she would always offer to make my favorite—fried egg and plantain with freshly made fried dumplings. My life as a cook began in Earlsfield, in the busy kitchen that belonged to my nan. It was a room frequently filled with the smell of cakes baking in her oven, and where fruits were always to be found soaking in a plastic jar filled to the brim with rum, neatly tucked in a corner cupboard alongside the mismatched crockery that kick-started my love affair with 1960s and '70s vintage homewares.

I've always been surrounded by matriarchs whose generosity is expressed by food—except my mum. Even though she didn't think she was, Mum was a great cook, but her generosity was felt through her presence; her energy made people feel safe. My nan, though, whenever any of her children were coming over, would always head to Wandsworth and buy a few extra hard dough breads, buns, or plantains to send them home with, along with some fried fish she'd just happened to make that day, us grandkids benefitting by association. Whenever I begged to stay over at my auntie's for dinner, she'd root through the fridge or freezer to see what food she could make stretch to feed us. These influential women gave (and continue to give) small, edible tokens of love, even without saying the words.

While my upbringing exposed me to Caribbean culture, it was the death of my big brother Richard that spurred me to start consciously engaging with my heritage. Before this tragedy, my active learning had been minimal. When I was at school, Black History Month was not the conscious affair it is now. That's an evolution I have mixed feelings about. In all honesty, I would rather see the contributions of my ancestors recognized and honored all year round. It's a disservice to everyone that they are not. We can't change the past, but we can certainly influence the future, and this starts by all of us understanding that history is shared. By taking ownership of that history, we can bring about real change.

After Richard's death, I wanted to be closer to my blackness as a way of being closer to the person I was when Richard was here—and to be closer to him, to the things we shared, to the things we loved. Food became the main vehicle for that connection. I remember Richard returning to college in Manchester and always taking back with him Tupperwares full of rice and peas to freeze. Just like him, I'd never learned to cook it—it was always Mum or Dad who made it for

us on a Sunday. I suddenly became acutely aware that our family recipes needed to be archived. By leaning into this task, I felt closer to my brother.

At this time, supper clubs were emerging as a way for people with diverse family heritages to explore and present their food on their own terms, with an authenticity that wasn't possible in restaurants. In 2016, I decided to start a supper club with my parents. It went by the name of Pop's Kitchen, and through it I hoped to celebrate and explore my Caribbean heritage. Pop's became the vehicle for healing and binding my family, after we'd spent six years flailing from the loss of my brother. (And here I am, writing a cookbook about family, community, and connection after losing another great—my mother. Once again, chaotically navigating my grief through food.)

In the UK, Caribbean cuisine has all too often been limited to take-out joints or high-end establishments. Pop's felt like a bridge between the two, and it also provided me with the space to carve out my own approach to the food. It led me to Joe and Biko, two cousins in East London, who were running a pop-up rum shop. They curated parties fueled by delicious—and lethal—punches and had been searching for a food partner. We started collaborating, and it soon became obvious that our events filled a gap. Caribbean spaces had declined heavily in the 1980s and 90s owing to gentrification, and active cultural erosion, leaving second- and third-generation Caribbean communities without places to retreat, relax, celebrate and, most importantly, feel safe.

The popularity of our events encouraged us to pour our energies into a new joint venture—Island Social Club. After many discussions, a lot of research and all the graphs Joe insisted upon, we launched a supper-club series, "Nyamming"—from the patois word nyam, meaning "food." Each event sought to bring chefs and performers together around a collaborative theme to further our guests' understanding of the Caribbean. The evenings were filled with carefully chosen food that we paired with exquisite rum cocktails, and challenging performances that prompted thoughtful conversations.

We were exploring the subtleties of the islands we love, honoring both their kinship and their variegation, and all the while we watched people connecting.

In time, Biko moved on, and Island Social Club began a year-long restaurant residency, where Joe and I continued to hold the Nyamming supper-club series, throwing parties and events and curating exhibitions at which artists could show their work. Later, the pandemic led Joe to pivot away from hospitality, but by then working with him and Biko had brought home to me the importance of community, of friends, and of other chosen family—as well as of the richness of my cultural heritage.

To me, the Caribbean is family; it's home, it's comfort, it's joy, and it's our way to bring people together through good food. Of course, Caribbean cuisine was one of the first global cuisines, borne out of the violent convergence of African, indigenous, and European cultures, with additional influences from South and East Asia and the Middle East. "Out of many, one people": the Jamaican national motto that so poetically defines Caribbeans. The depth and complexity of our cultural history is evident in our food, but while that complexity can't be ignored, it remains widely misunderstood, and our food seems a mystery to many. Prejudices and preconceptions are commonplace. Among the most frequent are that Caribbean dishes are only for those who love spicy food; that this food doesn't belong as "dinner-party food" and instead should be reserved for occasions when it can be dialed up to the same level as a heady sound system. Certainly, Caribbean dishes hold their own at Carnival, but they can also be subtle—spiced, not spicy, with complex flavors that derive from layers of freshly harvested ingredients.

You'll never step into a Caribbean home without being offered something to eat or drink—it's part of our culture. The breaking of bread can connect those with seemingly nothing in common, demolishing barriers and emphasizing unity and kinship rather than difference. Sharing is at the heart of my cooking, and it is at the heart of *Kin*.

Spices, Sauces, Pickles.

All too often the cuisine of the Caribbean, though rich with diverse flavors, is dismissed as suitable only for those who love spicy food. Yes, there are chiles— but often these chiles are deployed to add depth to a dish, and not solely for their heat. Chiles are nuanced—they can be sweet, floral, fruity, even smoky. It's possible to use them to offer up all these notes, with or without a peppery punch.

Not all Caribbean people love spicy food—many do, but plenty don't—so, just like those chiles, be nuanced and tailor their use to your taste. If you're not someone who enjoys much heat, either use them whole (pierced to prevent bursting), and remove them as they start to soften, or avoid using them at all. Scotch bonnets, those most characteristically fiery of Caribbean chiles, vary in heat depending on the conditions in which they've grown; my advice would always be to use less, then taste and adjust accordingly. Finally, if you have the patience, whole spices—toasted and then ground—will make a world of difference to your dishes. They add so much more flavor.

My Top Spice Mix (*adobo* in places with Spanish or Portuguese ties, from the Spanish word *adobar*, meaning "to marinate") is an all-purpose seasoning that knits together Caribbean cuisine. Such is its endless versatility, I use it in everything: in curries, in my jerk to season the meat before the marinade, in pastry for my patties. There are no hard-and-fast rules for what goes in. Key players, though, are paprika, onion, garlic, and some kind of dried chile. Store-bought varieties, while great when you're short on time, don't compare to a homemade batch. As for garam masala . . . I make so much curry that making my own curry spice mixes is a bit of a no-brainer (see also the Jamaican and Colombo curry powders, page 24). It's very speedy, and the food is so thankful for it. This garam masala—warm with a touch of sweetness; a symbol of the Indian influence on Caribbean cuisine—is a solid all-rounder, featuring in my Ital Chickpea Curry and Eggplant Curry (see pages 145 and 159, respectively).

SPICES, SAUCES, PICKLES

Top Spice Mix

¼ tsp black
   peppercorns
4 tsp cumin seeds
1 tsp fine sea salt
2 tbsp sweet smoked
   paprika
2 tsp onion powder
2 tsp garlic powder
1 tsp ground mild chiles
2 tsp dried oregano
¼ tsp yellow mustard
   powder

Toast the peppercorns and cumin seeds in a dry frying pan on low heat, for 2–3 minutes, or until they are fragrant. Immediately remove the toasted spices from the heat and tip them into a mortar or spice grinder along with the other ingredients. Pound them with the pestle, or turn on the grinder and pulse everything to a fine grain. To store, transfer the mixture to an airtight container. It will keep for up to six months.

Garam Masala

2 tbsp cumin seeds
1½ tbsp coriander
   seeds
1 tsp green cardamom
   seeds
1 tsp black peppercorns
2–2½ inches/5–6cm
   cinnamon stick
½ tsp fennel seeds
¼ tsp cloves
Pinch of grated
   nutmeg, or to taste

Toast all the ingredients except the nutmeg in a dry frying pan on low heat, for 2–3 minutes, or until they are fragrant. Immediately remove the toasted spices from the heat and tip them into a mortar or spice grinder. Pound them with the pestle, or turn on the grinder and pulse everything to a fine grain. Add the nutmeg according to your taste and mix in. To store, transfer the mixture to an airtight container. It will keep for up to six months.

Jamaican Curry Powder is called so because it uses pimento and a decent amount of ground turmeric, and doesn't contain dried chile—in many Caribbean curries, heat usually comes from adding fresh Scotch bonnet during cooking. When I started using this particular combination in my curry dishes, I noticed a greater complexity, which inevitably meant greater enjoyment. Colombo, also known as West Indian Curry Powder, contains toasted rice (brown rice will create a nuttier finish than white—but you choose), which provides a thickener, with the yellow mustard and greater use of fenugreek bringing the earthier notes, with a hint of spiciness from the mustard.

Jamaican Curry Powder

1 tbsp coriander seeds
1 tbsp cumin seeds
1 tbsp pimento berries
½ tsp black peppercorns
1½ tsp fenugreek seeds or ¾ tsp ground fenugreek seeds
3 arms from a star anise
2 tbsp ground turmeric

Toast all the ingredients in a dry frying pan on low heat, for 2–3 minutes, or until they are fragrant. Immediately remove the toasted spices from the heat and tip them into a mortar or spice grinder. Pound them with the pestle, or turn on the grinder and pulse them to a fine grain. To store, transfer the mixture to an airtight container. It will keep for up to six months.

Alternatively, you can combine the whole spices and store them unground—then, simply shake them up and take them out as you need to grind them. I prefer to grind before storing, as I usually make a small batch and use most of it at once or in a short amount of time.

Colombo Curry Powder

1 tbsp white or brown rice
1 tbsp cumin seeds
1 tbsp coriander seeds
2 tsp yellow mustard seeds
1 tsp black peppercorns
¼ tsp cloves
1 tbsp ground turmeric
1 tsp fenugreek seeds or ½ tsp ground fenugreek seeds

Toast the rice in a dry, small frying pan on medium heat for 5 minutes, or until it has taken on some color and it's smelling toasted. Set it aside on a plate.

Add all the remaining spices, except the ground fenugreek if that's what you're using (but include the seeds). Toast on medium heat for 3–5 minutes, until they are fragrant, then immediately tip the spices into a mortar or spice grinder, along with the toasted rice and ground fenugreek. Pound them with the pestle, or turn on the grinder and pulse to a fine grain. To store, transfer the mixture to an airtight container. It will keep for up to six months.

I love jerk—it features plenty in this book, and rightly so. It's a delicious example of the ways in which you can play with flavor in food. The opening sweet, earthy notes of pimento give way to the Scotch bonnet's heat, which builds as you eat. While it's specifically Jamaican, jerk is an incredible example of the complexity and ingenuity of Caribbean cuisine in general, and of how the food is so richly expressive of the people. This and the following two jerks are an introduction to its characteristic flavors.

I use this rub principally with a little oil to marinate meat, fish, and veggies, but it's also useful for layering flavor in jerk dishes, or adding dimension and complexity elsewhere—the sweet and smoky flavors pair particularly well with coconut-based recipes, such as my Ital Coconut Stew on page 147.

SPICES, SAUCES, PICKLES

Jerk Rub

2 x 3-inch/7.5cm
  cinnamon sticks
½ tsp coriander seeds
½ tsp cumin seeds
2 tsp pimento berries
½ tsp black
  peppercorns
1 tbsp dried thyme
1 tbsp onion powder
1 tbsp garlic powder
½ tsp grated nutmeg
2 tsp Scotch bonnet
  powder, or your
  preferred chile
  powder
½ tsp fine sea salt
  (optional)

Toast the cinnamon sticks, coriander and cumin seeds, pimento berries, and black peppercorns in a dry frying pan on low heat, for 2–3 minutes, or until they are fragrant. Immediately remove the toasted spices from the heat and tip them into a mortar or spice grinder with the remaining spices, and the salt (if using). Pound them with the pestle, or turn on the grinder and pulse them to your desired coarseness. To store, transfer the mixture to an airtight container. It will keep for up to six months.

Freshness brings variety and depth, which is why I'm obsessed with hammering it into my cooking. My jerk marinade features key flavor notes: pimento for earthy smokiness, Scotch bonnet for heat, and soy for saltiness and browning. These flavors pay homage to "jerking"—the traditional process of cooking meat, usually pork, slowly over pimento wood, with the meat marinated in spices with plenty of Scotch bonnet. The result is blackened skin with tender, flavored flesh. No two jerk marinades are the same. I like to add lots of herbs for maximum freshness, but if you prefer more punch, pull back on them. If you're looking for sweeter tones, add sugar, with a touch of citrus for balance. For the gluten-free gang, use tamari instead of soy—the extra two tablespoons will help achieve that same umami.

Jerk Marinade

⅔ cup/25g fresh thyme, stemmed, or 2 tbsp dried thyme
¾ cup/150g cilantro
6 onions, peeled and quartered
2 garlic heads, cloves separated and peeled
1 tbsp pimento berries
1 tbsp ground cinnamon
2 tsp grated nutmeg
¼ cup/60ml light or dark soy sauce (I prefer dark) or 6 tbsp/90ml tamari
6 Scotch bonnets, halved and seeded

Tip all the ingredients into a food processor and blitz until smooth, stopping occasionally to use a spatula to scrape down any of the mixture that has escaped the blades. The marinade will store in a sterilized jar in the fridge for up to two weeks. Or, you can decant it into ice-cube trays and pop it in the freezer for up to three months, defrosting as necessary (one cube is usually about 2 tablespoons, but check your own tray).

Jamaican at heart, Jamaican by nature, I have many of my own jerk seasonings and, to be extra, I am giving you not two, but three. You can use them together, separately or in any combination. The rub and marinade (see page 27 and page 28, respectively) work for the base, while this sauce is best suited to basting during cooking or glazing at the end of it, or as a sauce when you serve. The results create deep, full flavor. As a child I didn't do spice . . . in fact, I didn't do much flavor at all, but even I couldn't resist the pull of jerk on a barbecue. I may have, in the end, walked off with only a plain burger or sausage, but it was jerk that got me there in the first place. Feel free to experiment with my ingredients here—for example, if you're a fan, try adding ginger for its pungent warmth.

SPICES, SAUCES, PICKLES

Jerk Sauce

4–6 Scotch bonnets
2 small onions
8 garlic cloves, peeled
6 green onions
¼ cup/60ml apple
  cider vinegar
¼ cup/60ml light or
  dark soy sauce
  (I prefer dark) or
  6 tbsp/90ml tamari
1 tsp fine sea salt
1½ tsp black
  peppercorns
⅓ oz/10g ginger root
2 tbsp pimento berries
1 tsp grated nutmeg
10 thyme sprigs
2 tbsp sunflower oil
2 tbsp lime juice
1–3 tbsp dark brown
  sugar

Halve, then remove the seeds from the Scotch bonnets (how many you use will depend on your preference for heat). Place the halves, with all the remaining ingredients, but only 1 tablespoon of the sugar, in a food processor and blend until everything is as smooth as you can get it.

Transfer the mixture to a small frying pan and place the pan on medium heat. Cook for about 10 minutes, until the sauce has darkened toward a caramel color (turn down the heat if the sauce is bubbling too vigorously). If your sauce isn't darkening enough and you want a deeper caramel color, add the remaining sugar a little at a time, until you reach your desired color and flavor. Cool the sauce and transfer it to a sterilized jar to enjoy as needed. It will store in the fridge for about three months.

Mojo is a sour orange sauce traditionally used in Cuba, the largest of the Caribbean islands. It's here that, perhaps unsurprisingly given its history as a Spanish colony, you feel Spanish influence beyond the language alone. I found the use of spices significantly more tempered in Cuba than elsewhere in the Caribbean, with the food often giving sour or smoky notes instead. The heavy use of oregano and citrus offers both sweet and sour, and garlic is deployed without restraint—enough to make my heart swell (anywhere that uses garlic as liberally as I dare is forever a favorite). While the parallels to the rest of Caribbean are felt less keenly in Cuban food, they are strong in the culture, the music, and the energies. When I visited, I also found a real sense of Cuban "self"—it was infectious, and pulsing.

You can use mojo as a dipping sauce, as a marinade, or (if you're like me) to sample on a spoon. The souring of the orange is nothing short of genius—citrus can add so much dimension to a dish. Combining it with lemon and lime, as here, really lets each engage in a rhythm that balances so perfectly with the others.

SPICES, SAUCES, PICKLES

Mojo Sauce

1 garlic head (about 14 cloves)
2 tsp fine sea salt, plus extra if needed
1 tsp black peppercorns
2 tsp dried oregano
1 tsp ground cumin
¾ cup plus 2 tbsp/ 200ml freshly squeezed orange juice (about 3 large oranges)
7 tbsp/100ml lemon juice (2–3 lemons)
7 tbsp/100ml lime juice (3–4 limes)
4½ oz/125g onions (1–2 onions), minced
⅓ cup/80ml olive oil

Separate and peel the garlic cloves, then place them in a mortar along with the salt. Mash the two together with the pestle until you have a paste (or, you can do this in a small food processor). Transfer the mixture to a large jar.

Clean and dry out the mortar and pestle and grind the peppercorns to a coarse powder. Add this to the jar.

Add the remaining ingredients, close the lid tightly, and give the jar a good shake. Taste the sauce and adjust the seasonings if needed—it should be tangy and garlicky! Transfer the sauce to a sterilized jar. It will keep in the fridge for up to three months.

We have the Indo-Caribbean community to thank for chutneys in the Caribbean. Once slavery had been abolished, Indian people arrived via the indentured laborer system (really slavery by another name). Their culinary influence is strongest both in Guyana and in Trinidad and Tobago, but it extends all around the Caribbean islands.

To me, you cannot go wrong with something sweet and sticky with a touch of spice, and this chutney is addictive. Feel free to choose your heat—use anything from a sliver of Scotch bonnet to a whole one (just remember to seed it first)—and then serve the chutney enthusiastically, with everything. If you like to plan, make this a year ahead, allowing a good twelve months for the flavors to meld.

Mango Chutney

WITH A TOUCH (OR MORE) OF SCOTCHIE

1½ cups/360ml white wine vinegar

2 cups/400g granulated sugar

1 tsp cumin seeds

2 tsp coriander seeds

8 cloves

10 cardamom pods

¼ tsp mild chile powder

½ tsp ground turmeric

2 tsp fine sea salt

6 firm mangoes, peeled, pitted, and chopped into about ½-inch/1cm cubes

1 Scotch bonnet, seeded and finely chopped, or to taste

6 garlic cloves, roughly smashed

1½ oz/40g ginger root, peeled and finely chopped

2 tsp nigella seeds (celery or black sesame seeds both work well as a sub)

Pour the vinegar and sugar into a medium saucepan on medium–low heat, and heat until the sugar has dissolved. Then, increase the heat, and let it reduce until it becomes more syrupy—this should take no more than 6–8 minutes.

Meanwhile, toast the cumin seeds, coriander seeds, cloves, and cardamom pods in a dry frying pan on low heat, for 2–3 minutes, or until they are fragrant. Immediately remove the toasted spices from the heat and tip them into a mortar with the chile powder and ground turmeric. Remove the cardamom seeds from the pods and discard the pods, then use the pestle to grind the spices to your desired coarseness—a little bit of texture is fine. Alternatively, you can pulse the spices in a spice grinder, if you have one.

Add all the spices to the vinegar syrup, along with the salt, mango, Scotch bonnet, garlic, ginger, and nigella seeds. Cook for about 1½ hours, or until your chutney is thick and syrupy. Transfer the hot chutney to sterilized jars, pop on the lids, and let cool. Once cooled, the chutney can keep, unopened, for a couple of years.

People rarely associate pickling with Caribbean food, but the cuisine uses vinegar in very similar ways to the West. On board slave ships, with limited foods available, souring wine was a way to halt rotting and make what food there was last longer.

In the Caribbean, you'll often see pickled vegetables served with fish or seafood, as their sweetness and saltiness marry well. One of my favorite combinations is these pickled green onions with Pepper Shrimp (see page 64), but you also see it with Fried Fish Escovitch (see page 87).

SPICES, SAUCES, PICKLES

Pickled Green Onions

½ cup/120ml apple cider vinegar

3 tbsp light brown sugar

1 tsp fine sea salt

¼ cup/60ml water

1 bunch of green onions, trimmed and sliced

1 tsp mustard seeds

Combine the vinegar, brown sugar, salt, and water in a small saucepan on medium–low heat. Once the mixture is at a rolling boil, turn the heat down to a simmer and add the green onions and mustard seeds. Stir to combine and cook for 2–3 minutes. Then, take the pan off the heat and let the onions cool. Place the liquid and onions into a sterilized jar, if you wish, and keep for up to four weeks in fridge— although they rarely last that long for me!

A delicious, fresh sauce, green seasoning is the foundation of so many Caribbean dishes. Versions vary according to ingredient availability and locale, of course. In Trinidad and Tobago, using fresh chadon beni (also known as Mexican cilantro, culantro, or long cilantro) is paramount; in Spanish-speaking countries, tomatoes go in and the sauce is cooked and called *sofrito*. I like a combination of parsley and cilantro—or, if I can find it, chadon beni, which is more fragrant (use a third of the amount given for cilantro and check for flavor before adding more). Try a range of green herbs, as well as onion, garlic, and your choice of sweet pepper. I adore the sweetness of a pimento, which lends a very gentle heat on par with a pinch of black pepper—but it can be hard to find, so you could easily swap it for a Romano red pepper. Scotch bonnet adds a lovely fruitiness, but don't include it if you're worried about heat. You might notice that the results are not always as green as you'd expect—that's okay. The color will depend on the size of your ingredients, and, anyway, it's the flavor that counts.

SPICES, SAUCES, PICKLES

Green Seasoning

½ cup/30g cilantro
⅔ cup/15g flat-leaf parsley
½ celery stalk
2 large green onions
1 pimento pepper (cherry pepper) or ½ Romano pepper, seeded
2 shallots, peeled
4 garlic cloves, peeled
⅓ cup/15g thyme, stemmed
1 Scotch bonnet, halved and seeded (optional)
1–2 tbsp water or olive oil

Roughly chop both the leaves and the stems of the cilantro and the parsley, roughly chop the celery, spring onions, and pimento or Romano pepper, and then quarter or halve (depending on size) the shallots.

Add all these chopped herbs, spices, and vegetables with the rest of the ingredients and 1 tablespoon of the water or olive oil to a food processor and blitz to a very finely chopped marinade—add the remaining water or oil if the mixture needs a little help to become fully chopped. The marinade will store in an airtight container in the fridge for up to one week. Or, you can decant it into ice-cube trays and pop it in the freezer for up to three months, defrosting as necessary (one cube is usually about 2 tablespoons, but check your own tray).

Chow chow is a thin-skinned squash also known as christophene or chayote (it gets the name chow chow—my personal favorite—from India). My dad hates it . . . why, I don't know, because I find the subtle, cucumber-like flavor simply absorbs all the flavors thrown at it. This pickle adds such a welcome bite to salads or when served alongside a creamy, spicy curry. I might add some tomatoes to the chow chow when they're in season—as with the vinegar, they are a match made in heaven. Always buy chow chow with bright green skin—lots of dark spots or excessively wrinkled skin means the vegetable is a little past its peak, although you can find chow chows that are bumpy-skinned and those are fine.

SPICES, SAUCES, PICKLES

Pickled Chow Chow

1 chow chow, peeled, quartered and cored
1 carrot, peeled
1¼ cups/300ml apple cider vinegar
6 black peppercorns
1 bay leaf
1 star anise
1 tsp fine sea salt
6 tbsp/75g granulated sugar
¾ cup plus 2 tbsp/200ml water

If you have a mandoline (take care, I'm terrified of the things—if you like your fingers, use a guard or glove), attach a shredding blade and shred the chow chow into a mixing bowl. Then repeat for the carrot. If you don't have a mandoline and are using a paring knife, cut your chow chow quarters into equal sizes and slice each piece thinly. Stack the slices on top of each other, then cut downward thinly again—you should have some lovely matchsticks. Repeat for the carrot. Transfer the chow chow and carrot equally to clean, sterilized jam jars (about three or four should do it) and set aside.

Add the remaining ingredients to a small saucepan. Place the pan on low heat and stir until your salt and sugar have dissolved.

Remove the pan from the heat and pour the pickling liquid over the vegetables until they are submerged. Let rest for 1 hour, then your pickles are ready to use— but you can let them pickle for longer, if you prefer. They will keep, unopened, in the fridge for two weeks.

I like to serve a choice of dips when serving my fritters, a trio to be precise. There's nothing more satisfying than seeing a plate streaked with sauces, mixed with scraps of fried things left behind. So, here and on the following page are my three favorites. First, Hot Pepper Sauce. I love spice. I enjoy how it feels adventurous, even mischievous in the way it can creep in. This hot sauce is actually a middle ground—one for those who don't want pepper sauce to ruin them, with the chow chow softening the intensity of the heat. You can easily make it punchier if you prefer hot-hot—just add more Scotch bonnets or include a few of the seeds. Serve it over everything, like my dad does. For me, the Ginger Chile Sauce on page 43 is right up there, a bridge on the path to hot sauce and second only to . . . ketchup. I'm a sucker for the red stuff. The Spiced Ketchup is my love letter to tommy K (as we've lovingly nicknamed it in the UK) and, if you're not into hot pepper sauces (I am) or mayo (I'm not) or regular tomato ketchup (why?), this is your perfect condiment for everything. Developed initially to serve inside a Coco Bread Bun with "Shark" Hake Bites (see pages 182 and 70, respectively), it is a great accompaniment if you want some extra body over the store-bought stuff.

SPICES, SAUCES, PICKLES

Hot Pepper Sauce

½ chow chow, quartered
1 red bell pepper, seeded
3–5 Scotch bonnets (depending on heat preference), seeded
4 garlic cloves, peeled
7 tbsp/100ml red wine vinegar
1 tsp fine sea salt, plus extra to season
1 tbsp dark brown sugar
7 tbsp/100ml water
Ground black pepper

Bring a small saucepan of salted water to a boil on high heat, then pop in your chow chow. Boil the chow chow for 15–20 minutes, until soft enough that you can pierce it with a sharp knife without pressure, then drain it and pop it into a food processor.

While the chow chow is cooking, roughly chop the bell pepper and Scotch bonnets and set aside. Then, once the chow chow is ready, put them with the garlic into the food processor with the cooked chow chow and blitz until everything is finely chopped.

Transfer the mixture to a small pan, along with the vinegar, salt, sugar, and water. Stir and place on medium–low heat. Bring to a boil, then lower the heat and simmer for about 15 minutes—the sauce should have reduced to a thicker consistency and the vinegar should have lost its sharpness. Taste and season with salt and pepper and add a dash more water to loosen, if needed. When you're happy with the flavor and consistency, take the pan off the heat and let the sauce cool. Blitz again until smooth and transfer the sauce to a sterilized jar. It will keep, unopened, in the fridge for up to three months.

Ginger Chile Sauce

½–1 Scotch bonnet, seeded

1 large red bell pepper, seeded

1½ oz/40g ginger root, peeled

4 garlic cloves, peeled

⅔ cup/160ml apple cider vinegar

1¼ cups/240g granulated sugar

1 tsp/4g powdered pectin

Pinch of salt

Roughly chop the Scotch bonnet, red bell pepper, and ginger and pop them in a food processor with the garlic. Blitz until finely chopped.

Place the vinegar, sugar, pectin, and salt in a small saucepan on medium–low heat and stir until your sugar has dissolved. Scrape the Scotch bonnet mixture into the pan, stir, then turn up the heat and bring everything to a boil. Then, immediately lower the heat to a simmer, scraping off and discarding any scum that appears on the top. Cook for 25–30 minutes, until the mixture reduces by about half and becomes syrupy. A quick way to check the jam is ready is to take a small amount and pop it on a plate and place it in the fridge, give it a minute or two, then test—it's ready if it's a jammy texture that's nice and sticky. If not, cook for another minute or two and test again, repeating until you're happy.

Transfer the sauce to a sterilized jar and keep it somewhere dark for up to six months. Once you crack into it, keep it in the fridge for up to four weeks.

Spiced Ketchup

1 tbsp olive oil

1 small onion, finely chopped

3 garlic cloves, sliced

2 tbsp light brown sugar

½ tsp sweet smoked paprika

¼ tsp ground pimento

¼ tsp ground cloves

3 tbsp white wine vinegar

1 tbsp tomato paste

14 oz/400g roma tomatoes

½ tsp fine sea salt, or to taste

¼ tsp ground black pepper, or to taste

Heat the olive oil in a small saucepan on medium heat. When hot, add the onion and garlic and cook on low heat for 3–4 minutes, until softened (just make sure the garlic doesn't burn). Add your sugar, paprika, pimento, and cloves and cook for about 1 minute, until the sugar melts—keep an eye on it as you don't want it to burn.

As soon as the sugar has melted, add the vinegar and tomato paste and cook on medium heat for no more than 3 minutes, until the vinegar has reduced; you'll notice the mixture thickening. Add your tomatoes, breaking them up with a wooden spoon, and bring the liquid to a simmer. Cook, stirring occasionally, for 15–20 minutes, until the tomatoes have started to soften and break down.

Transfer the mixture to a food processor and blitz until smooth. Season with the salt and pepper to taste and pour into a sterilized jar. The ketchup will store, unopened, in the fridge for up to six months, and three months once opened.

We make.

When you're at life's crossroads, you become far more attuned to things you might have once taken for granted. For me, that's been my body. I've become very conscious of its workings—most of all, how it props me up from day to day, in a multitude of ways. It tells me if I've neglected to provide it with food and water. It forces me to rest when I'm trying to push through my exhaustion. It's also incredibly intuitive. We walk by taking steps. We dance by hearing music. Once our bodies have learned these actions, we can do them without thought.

Whenever I'm lost in a job where muscle memory takes over—making bread or roti, crushing spices I've toasted, decanting sauces into jars—I find myself focusing on my hands. They both lead me in life, and bond me to my identity. In processes so simple, I'm free to get lost, and it's there I most often find peace. Food—it's how I express myself, my most creative outlet. All forms of creation have value (magic is often waiting in the mistakes), but nothing feeds my soul more than when those who eat my food say they can sense that it was made with love.

So much of who I am came through osmosis. Watching my nan in her kitchen; weekend shopping trips with Mum; helping Dad cook Sunday dinner. Foodways provide opportunity, offering space for the exchange of information between generations and within communities. After a recent event that I'd catered, a guest messaged me on social media to ask for one of the recipes. I could have told them to wait for this book, I guess, but my instinct was immediately to share— or rather, guide, as I've been taught to by my family; we rarely have a proper recipe, it's more likely a little of this and a touch of that. After all, the guest's motivation was to replicate and continue traditions that are centered around community and kinship.

When I had my daughter, my impulse to share my heritage and traditions grew even stronger; it affirmed who I wanted to be. It's as though the otherness I have often felt, owing to my blackness or to not being "Black enough," had not gone away but instead shifted. I was desperate to fit in—I'm now very comfortable not to. There isn't one way of being, and I'm keen for my daughter to understand that, too. I will never know the world through Marcie's eyes, but I can do my best to make sure that the experiences I share with her affirm her in who she already is, and strengthen her sense of cultural identity. And so, I hope, the cycle will continue.

All human history is rooted in Africa. That's where the first food came from, and its traces are present in today's cooking, notably in the African-derived foodways of the Caribbean, Latin American, and North American cuisines. It's why we see multiple regional variations of the same dish—take the Ghanaian *waakye*, a dish made of cooked rice and beans (characteristically red) and flavored by sorghum leaf, found in both Africa and Asia. *Waakye* is often credited as the dish from which Jamaican rice and peas (see page 117), Guyana's cookup rice, and Cuban Moros y Cristianos (see page 118) originated, as well as plenty more rice and bean dishes found within the diaspora. *Waakye*, a word from the Hausa language meaning "beans," is a shortform of the name *shinkafa da wake*, which translates as rice and beans. When cooking it, black-eyed peas are most often used, which may go some way to explaining why, in the Caribbean, we often refer to beans as peas. Several of the countries that were flagged up on an ancestry test that I took a few years ago related to the Hausa people, native to West and Central Africa. Although these DNA tests are anything but perfect in locating where we come from, they do highlight the idea of borders as false, entirely political constructs, serving to blind us to the fact that we are one common humanity.

Africa may be the continent of my ancestors, but Jamaica is the land of my people. The map that came with my DNA results suggested that I am *very* Jamaican, the lines criss-crossing the Atlantic Ocean between Jamaica and West Africa pointing to the building blocks of me. Prior to the transatlantic slave trade, food was a central means of cultural expression for African people, a declaration of communal, social, and familial ties, and even with the introduction of spices and other food commodities brought by early European traders, these were absorbed into traditions that already existed, rather than replacing them. If anything, African foods had a stronger influence on European diets than the other way around. The continuing strength of these traditions is a testament to the resilience of those who were enslaved, who withstood the most disruptive and dehumanizing of experiences.

Nothing exemplifies this better than jerk, which stemmed from survival-based cooking, and the utilization of scarce resources. The Taínos, who described Jamaica as the "land of wood and water," inhabited the island before the Spanish arrived in 1494, and learned to cook meat in pits to avoid capture by the Europeans. Previously they had cooked over pimento wood on grills known as *barbacoa*—the word translates as "heated sticks." They would hunt wild boar and spice the meat, before cooking it over a low fire. "Jerking" the meat preserved it for longer.

Under the British, who invaded Jamaica in 1655, conditions were brutal, and those slaves who managed to escape would join communities of free "maroons" in the island's mountainous interior, where cooking in fire pits was necessary to avoid detection. This is how the cooking practices of the Taínos combined with those of the Africans, and the modern dish we know today as jerk was conceived. Many communities around the island cook jerk this way, heavily spiced with pimento and Scotch bonnet, cooking low and slow over a smoldering fire to yield tender meat. Nowadays, most people use sauces or marinades—some bought, others homemade— that simulate the flavors of fire, honoring the tradition in a different way.

Snacks, Fritters, Tarts.

Snacks are often sold on the side of the road in the
Caribbean—smoky grilled corn protected by its husk,
or plantain crisps or pepper shrimp in little plastic bags.
I'm someone who likes warm food, even in hot weather,
and this preference extends to snacks. I would never turn
down a salty chip—not ever—but I prefer to think of
my snacks as mini meals. In this chapter are some of my
favorite dishes, lending themselves to shared eating and
celebration—I won't judge, though, if you wish
to whip them up for one. (Sharing with yourself is not
only valid, but encouraged.) If you want to serve them
as mains, simply double or triple the quantities.

By the way, all these dishes are designed to be eaten
with one hand. I'm an expressive person and a lot
of that comes from rather overactive gesticulation.
I was never one to be dainty—this is the kind of
eating I was designed to do. Oh, and patties are
never better than when you eat them from a paper
bag, crumbs collecting at the bottom for a last taste
of that divine crumbly pastry. (I derive a lot of pleasure
from crumbs, a gift that keeps on giving!)

Patties are nostalgia for me—seeing them in neatly stacked rows at my favorite take-away shops, asking for them in shy, hushed tones, a microwave pinging, a disposable napkin and a paper bag that turns opaque against the buttery pastry. Patties remind me of errands, of comfort, and of home. Even now, these are my soul food on-the-go, lending themselves to being eaten one-handed. I'm offering two fillings here—the more readily engaged with veggie pattie, and (all hail the underdog) the chicken pattie, the outsider, the non-star of the show—until now.

SNACKS, FRITTERS, TARTS

Jamaican Patties

Makes ten to twelve

For the pastry
4 cups/500g all-
   purpose flour
1 tbsp ground turmeric
2 tsp Jamaican Curry
   Powder (page 24)
¼ tsp Top Spice Mix
   (page 23)
1 tsp fine sea salt
½ cup plus 2 tbsp/
   150g unsalted butter
¼ cup/50g shortening
½ cup/120ml ice-cold
   water
2 tsp apple cider
   vinegar
1 egg, beaten, or
   2 tbsp oat milk

For the veggie filling
1 tbsp olive oil, plus
   extra if needed
1 small onion, diced
1 tsp Top Spice Mix
   (page 23)
¼ tsp ground black
   pepper
½ tsp ground pimento
½ tsp Jamaican Curry
   Powder (page 24)
½ tsp ground turmeric
¼ tsp fine sea salt

For the chicken filling: Start the filling ahead of time. In a bowl, massage the chicken pieces with the salt, top spice, and curry powder. Cover the bowl, and refrigerate for at least 4 hours, but preferably overnight.

For the pastry: Add the flour, turmeric, curry powder, top spice, salt, butter, and shortening to a food processor and pulse slowly to a breadcrumb consistency. Add half of the cold water along with the vinegar and pulse until a dough starts to form (avoid overworking the dough). One table-spoon at a time, add the remaining water, until your pastry will hold together with a pinch. If you don't have a processor, combine by hand. Make sure everything is as cold as possible, engage frugally with the dough, and add the water slowly (you may not need it all). Empty the dough onto a lightly floured work surface and form it into a ball—the less you can handle the dough, the better. Wrap it in plastic wrap and then refrigerate until chilled (30–40 minutes). Meanwhile, make your chosen filling.

For the veggie filling: Heat the oil in a medium frying pan (one with a lid) on medium heat. Add the onion and cook for 5–7 minutes, until softened. Add your spices, salt, and garlic and fry for 1 minute, or until fragrant, adding a little water if it looks as though the mixture might burn. Add the carrot, bell pepper, and squash, then the hot sauce (if using) and stock and bring to a boil. Turn down the heat to a rolling simmer and cook until the stock has almost evaporated, adding the corn and peas for the last few minutes of cooking time. Fold in your breadcrumbs and green onions, then transfer the filling to a clean baking sheet, let cool, and cover and chill until cold (about 1 hour in total—a baking sheet allows for quicker cooling than a bowl).

1 garlic clove, finely
  chopped
1 small carrot,
  finely diced
½ red bell pepper,
  seeded and
  finely diced
2½ oz/75g butternut
  squash flesh, finely
  diced
1¼ cups/300ml
  vegetable stock
⅓ cup/50g frozen or
  drained canned corn
⅓ cup/50g frozen peas
⅓ cup/30g fresh
  breadcrumbs
2 green onions,
  thinly sliced

For the chicken filling
10½ oz/300g skinless,
  boneless chicken
  thighs, diced into
  ½-inch/1cm pieces
½ tsp fine sea salt,
  plus extra to season
1 tsp Top Spice Mix
  (page 23)
1½ tsp Jamaican Curry
  Powder (page 24)
1–2 tbsp sunflower oil
1 small onion, diced
4 garlic cloves,
  finely chopped
¼ oz/8g ginger root,
  peeled and diced
1 tsp thyme leaves
¼ Scotch bonnet,
  seeded and finely
  chopped (optional)
½ cup/120ml chicken
  stock
A handful of frozen
  corn kernels
2 tsp unsalted butter
¼ cup/20g fresh
  breadcrumbs
3 green onions, sliced
Ground black pepper

For the chicken filling: Remove the marinated chicken from the fridge and let it come up to room temperature. Heat 1 tablespoon of the oil in a medium frying pan (one with a lid), on medium–high heat. Add the chicken and turn it for a few minutes, until brown all over. Remove the chicken from the pan and set it aside on a plate.

Add another 1 tablespoon of oil to your pan, if needed, decrease the heat to medium and add the onion. Cook for 5–7 minutes, until softened. Add your garlic, ginger, and thyme leaves, as well as your Scotch bonnet, if you like a little heat, and cook for another minute or two.

Add your chicken back to the pan, along with your stock, and stir. Bring the liquid to a boil, then place the lid on the pan and lower the heat. Simmer for 10 minutes, then remove the lid. Add the corn and cook until most of the stock has evaporated (you don't want it completely dry). Then, turn off the heat, add your butter, and let it melt before folding in your breadcrumbs and green onions. Season to taste with salt and pepper, then transfer the mixture to a baking sheet until completely cooled.

To assemble the patties: Protect your work surface with parchment paper to avoid the dough staining it, then dust your rolling pin with a little flour. Remove the ball of dough from the fridge and lightly press it with the palm of your hand to flatten it. Using the rolling pin, roll out your pastry to a rough circle about ⅛ inch/3mm thick. At any point if you think the pastry is getting too warm, chill it and come back to it. Using a 6-inch/15cm plate or bowl as a guide, with a sharp knife cut out ten pastry circles from the dough. You can ball and re-roll your dough, but it's best to do this only once.

One at a time, spoon about 2 tablespoons of your chosen filling into each pastry round, leaving a ½-inch/1cm border around the edge. Wet the edge of one half of each disc with the beaten egg or oat milk (reserve the remainder to glaze later) and fold over the pastry to create a parcel. Press the edges together with your fingers to seal, then press with a fork to create pleats. Transfer the patties to a baking sheet lined with parchment paper and chill them for 10–15 minutes, while you preheat your oven to 350°F. (Or, you can freeze the patties, then cook from frozen, extending the cooking time accordingly.)

Brush the patties with your remaining beaten egg or oat milk, then bake them for 30 minutes, or until deep golden and piping hot. Let them cool for 5 minutes before serving with Hot Pepper Sauce, or go for the double carb and enjoy one between a Coco Bread Bun (see page 182).

51

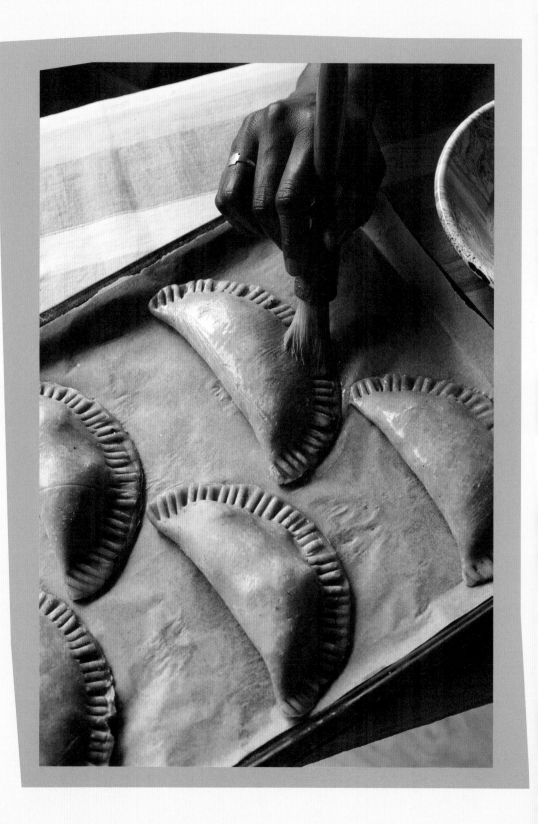

My parents were born in Jamaica, and ackee and saltfish is the island's national dish. Salty fish and creamy fruit might not suggest tasty, but they are—trust me. Saltfish is most often salt-cured, dried cod, but also frequently other meaty white fish. A protein lifeline introduced during colonization, it is now embedded in Caribbean food. I came to ackee and saltfish later than I care to admit, but these days I cherish both cooking and eating it, the smell conjuring up a sense of the ordinary made precious. I love to make it into tarts—served with a green salad with Pineapple and Lime Dressing (see page 109), they make for a delicious starter. Alternatively, you can make just the filling and pair it more traditionally with dumplings (see page 181) and fried or boiled plantain (see pages 58 and 120), for a breakfast of champions.

SNACKS, FRITTERS, TARTS

Ackee & Saltfish Tarts

Makes six

For the pastry
½ quantity of pattie
    pastry (page 50),
    chilled

For the filling
3½ oz/100g saltfish
½ tbsp olive oil
1 onion, finely
    chopped
¼ Scotch bonnet,
    seeded and
    finely chopped
3 thyme sprigs,
    stemmed
¾ tsp ground
    black pepper
2 tomatoes, diced
½ cup/165g drained
    ackee
Lime wedges
    (optional), to serve

Rinse the saltfish, then soak it overnight in cold water in the fridge. Discard the soaking water and place it in boiling water to soften. Taste a pinch of the fish to check the salt levels—if it's still too salty, soak it for another 5 minutes in warm water and check again. Once you're happy, shred the fish into flakes. Preheat the oven to 400°F and grease and flour six 4-inch/10cm individual tart pans.

Remove the chilled pastry from the fridge. Dust your rolling pin with a little flour and lightly press the ball of dough with the palm of your hand to flatten it. Roll out your pastry to a rough circle about ⅛ inch/4mm thick, then, using a 5-inch/12cm pastry cutter, cut out six circles, re-balling and rolling the pastry trimmings just once, if necessary. Press the pastry circles into your tart pans, trimming the excess. Line each tart shell with a piece of scrunched-up parchment paper and baking beans and blind bake the shells for 15 minutes, until lightly golden. Remove the beans and paper and return the shells to the oven for 10 minutes, until crisp and golden. Set aside, but leave the oven on.

Finish the filling: Heat the olive oil in a frying pan on medium heat. Cook the onion for 5–7 minutes, until softened, then add your Scotch bonnet, thyme and pepper. Cook for 2–3 minutes, add your tomatoes and flaked saltfish, and cook again for 2–3 minutes. Add your ackee and cook for just 1–2 minutes more (the tomatoes and ackee should hold their shape). Take the pan off the heat and split the mixture equally among the tart shells. Bake the filled tarts for 5 minutes to warm through, then serve with lime wedges for squeezing over the top, if you like.

We didn't have any Afro-Caribbean grocery stores in the immediate vicinity of home—it was sleepy and residential—so to avoid frequent twenty-minute drives to satisfy a craving for plantain chips, Mum stocked up when she went to her hairdresser in Tooting. The only problem was, she and I would polish them all off within a couple of days. I like to tell myself that Dad and my brother Richie weren't as interested in plantain chips as the two of us, but in truth I'm pretty certain they just never stood a chance. I'm proud to say my daughter is now the same—it's a cultural nugget passed from grandmother to granddaughter by way of lineage and legacy. I find comfort in that.

SNACKS, FRITTERS, TARTS

Plantain Chips

For four

2 green plantains,
   thinly sliced
Sunflower oil,
   for deep-frying
Fine sea salt,
   for sprinkling

The starches from plantain can leave a residue on your hands, so before you begin rub your hands with a little oil to create a barrier. Cut off the ends of one plantain, then score the skin, making four incisions along the seams—use the blade of a paring knife to get under the skin, moving down the length gently so as not to cut the plantain flesh. If you don't have a paring knife, use a small kitchen knife for the incisions, then a dinner knife to pry the skin away. Once you have removed the first section of skin, remove the remaining three sections with your finger (if this is a struggle, use the knife). Repeat to remove all the skin, then repeat the whole process for the second plantain.

Use a mandoline or the slicer of a food processor to cut the plantains into chips, $\frac{1}{16}$–$\frac{1}{8}$ inch/ 2–3mm thick. You're aiming for uniformity. For the crispest results, place your plantain slices in a bowl of cold, salted water for 30 minutes, then drain the slices and pat them dry.

Half-fill a deep, wide saucepan with sunflower oil and place it on medium heat. Once hot (about 374°F/190°C on a cooking thermometer; or use the wooden-spoon test on page 244), fry the chips in batches, separating them as you add them to the oil to avoid them sticking together as they cook, for 30–40 seconds per batch, or until golden. Remove each batch with a slotted spoon, transferring to a plate lined with paper towels to drain away the excess oil, and repeat until all the slices are cooked.

Sprinkle the chips with salt to serve. They'll stay fresh in an airtight container for up to three days.

Plantain has its roots in Asia, before coming to Africa, Europe, and the Caribbean through movement and trade. It grew in abundance in the Caribbean, providing a cheap, filling, and versatile provision. Nowadays, I feel it is one of the most important examples of a food that demonstrates the creativity of my people. The best use of a plantain depends on its ripeness. Green plantain is great for chips (see page 57), yellow is good for roasting, and blackened is perfect for frying. Blackened skin is a sign of goodness—I eat my plantain on the edge of moldy. You don't have to go that far and, in all honesty, plantains are tricky to cut when that ripe, but my gosh those sugars are worth it. For this recipe, look for yellow plantains that have black spots and that are still slightly firm to the touch (black spots alone can be a sign of bruising). I prefer to buy them all yellow, allowing them to ripen further in a fruit bowl.

Fried plantain is mighty fine on its own—but a squeeze of lime and a sprinkle of this lime and Scotch bonnet salt can turn something special into something exceptional.

SNACKS, FRITTERS, TARTS

Fried Plantain

WITH LIME & SCOTCH BONNET SALT

For two

1 yellow plantain
Sunflower oil,
 for deep-frying
Lime wedges
 (optional),
 for squeezing

For the salt
1 Scotch bonnet,
 halved and seeded
2 limes, zest only
¼ cup/60g fine sea salt

First, make the salt. Preheat your oven to 275°F and line a baking sheet with parchment paper. Pulse the Scotch bonnet, lime zest, and salt in a food processor until combined. Spread the mixture over the lined baking sheet, and place it in your oven for 30 minutes to dry out. I give it a stir every 5–10 minutes. Turn the oven off and let the salt cool inside for a few hours, or overnight if you have time. When you remove it, break up any clumps, then store the salt in glass jars. It'll keep indefinitely.

For the plantain, cut off the ends and score the skin once or twice so that it slides off easily. If, for any reason, the skin doesn't slide off, use the edge of your knife to release a corner and then your fingers to release the rest. Quarter the plantain lengthwise, then cut each quarter into ½-inch/1cm pieces, slightly on the diagonal to give you nice, crispy edges.

Half-fill a medium frying pan with sunflower oil and place it on medium heat. Once hot (about 374°F/190°C on a cooking thermometer; or use the wooden-spoon test on page 244), fry your plantain in batches for about 2 minutes on each side, or until nicely golden all over. Transfer each batch to a plate lined with paper towels to drain away the excess oil and repeat until all your plantain is cooked. Serve the plantain piled high in a small bowl, with lime squeezed over the top (if using), and sprinkled with the flavored salt.

For me, jerk pork conjures up images of a person beside an oil-drum grill, basting and rotating meat, and moving it to warmer or cooler sections depending on the stage of cooking. I see smoke wafting into surrounding spaces to signal that good food is coming. The patient waiting as your tummy rumbles is all part of the jerk experience. These bites are sweet, sticky, spicy, and irresistible, and I love to have them as a snack, but if you cook the pork whole, you can serve larger pieces as a meal. Double up the quantities to have it as a main—if you're lucky, there may be leftovers.

SNACKS, FRITTERS, TARTS

Naughty Pork Bites

For four

1 lb 2 oz/500g skin-on pork belly
1 tsp rock or fine sea salt, plus extra for sprinkling
1 tbsp Jerk Rub (page 27, optional)
2 tbsp Jerk Marinade (page 28)
A handful of cilantro (optional), roughly chopped, to serve

Score the pork skin in a criss-cross pattern, with cuts ½ inch/1cm apart—take care not to cut into the flesh. If you're cooking the pork in the oven, chop it into 1-inch/2.5cm pieces; if you're cooking on the barbecue, leave it whole.

Transfer the pork to a roasting dish, making sure there is plenty of room between the pieces, if relevant. Using your hands, massage the salt into the pork pieces, then do the same with the jerk rub (if using), and finally with the jerk marinade. Cover the roasting pan with foil and marinate the pork in the fridge overnight, or for up to 48 hours. Remove the meat from the fridge 30 minutes before cooking, so that it can come up to room temperature.

To cook in an oven: Preheat the oven to 425°F. Make sure all the fat on the pieces is facing upward, then re-cover the meat with foil. Cook for 10 minutes, then turn down the heat to 350°F and cook for 2 hours. Carefully remove the foil, baste the pork with the fat and sauce in the pan, and bake it, uncovered, for 30 minutes, or until it is soft, sticky, and tender. Allow it to rest, covered, for 20 minutes before serving sprinkled with sea salt and the cilantro (if using).

To cook on a barbecue: Once your barbecue is hot, move the coals to one side to create a cool zone. Lay the pork skin-side down on the coolest part, cover with a lid and cook for 20 minutes, or until crisp—take care not to let the skin burn. Turn the pork over, replace the lid, and cook it in the cool zone until it is tender enough to pull apart with a fork (about 2 hours). Once ready, remove the meat from the grill, cover it with foil, and allow it to rest for 30 minutes, before chopping it into pieces, and sprinkling with sea salt and the cilantro (if using), to serve.

I've guarded this little recipe of mine for a long time. It was the first recipe I ever developed and the starter at my first supper club—my "food baby." I've featured it in many a menu since then and it's still one of my favourites to this day. Fried spiced batter is food of the gods, which is why versions of fritters exist around the Caribbean and indeed the world. These fritters are an evolution of akara, native to West Africa, a version made from either black-eyed peas or cow beans. On special occasions, the beans are swapped out for fish or cassava; the saltfish version is a bedrock of the cuisine. These fritters are a homage to the fritters I would see among epic spreads in church halls, alongside big trays with Fried Fish Escovitch (see page 87), dumplings, and stews. They are little (or big) fried gods of delight.

SNACKS, FRITTERS, TARTS

My Saltfish Fritters

For four
(12–16 fritters)

5¼ oz/150g saltfish
1 cup plus 3 tbsp/150g
  all-purpose flour
1¾ tsp baking powder
¼ tsp Top Spice Mix
  (page 23)
¼ tsp ground black
  pepper
2¼ tsp Jamaican Curry
  Powder (page 24)
¼ tsp chile powder
  (your choice of heat,
  optional)
1 tbsp thyme leaves
  or 1 tsp dried thyme
¼ Scotch bonnet,
  seeded and
  finely chopped
2–3 green onions,
  finely chopped
¾ cup plus 2 tbsp/
  200ml water
Sunflower oil,
  for deep-frying
Hot Pepper Sauce
  (page 40, optional),
  to serve

Rinse the saltfish, then soak it overnight in cold water in the fridge. Discard the soaking water and place the fish in boiling water to soften. When you're ready to cook, taste a pinch of the fish to check the salt levels—if it's still too salty, soak it for another 5 minutes in warm water and check again (go carefully as you don't want to lose all the saltiness). Once you're happy, drain away the water again and use your hands to break the fish into flakes, at the same time making sure there aren't any bones. Set aside.

In a mixing bowl, combine the flour, baking powder, and the spice mix, black pepper, curry and chile powders, and thyme. Add the Scotch bonnet, green onions, and flaked saltfish and mix everything together thoroughly. Little by little, add the water, mixing well to make sure you've incorporated all the flour, until the batter reluctantly drops off the spoon (you might not need all the water—you don't want it too runny).

Half-fill a large frying pan with sunflower oil and heat it on medium heat. Once the oil is hot, drop in a small spoonful of the batter—if it sizzles, the oil is ready. Taste test the cooked batter to check for seasoning, adjusting if necessary. Using two large spoons (one to scoop and one to scrape off the batter into the oil), fry your fritters in batches of about three or four at a time for 2–3 minutes each side, until golden and crispy. Set each batch aside to drain on paper towels, while you fry the remainder. Serve with Hot Pepper Sauce for dipping, if you like.

I was late to the party with fish and seafood, so I've been making up for lost time with these pepper shrimp. In Jamaica, they are often served as snacks, in little plastic bags from the side of the road, usually with the shell on (here, I'm serving them shelled, but have given the alternative at the end of the method). They pack a flavorful punch, with a sauce that will have you mopping the bowl. If, for some reason, you don't use all your sauce, it's delicious as the base for a soup, adding in more shrimp or rice. Just don't waste it, it's too good. Use as good a quality white wine vinegar as you can—it makes a big difference to the flavor. I prefer to use that and a squeeze of lime in place of salt here, but if you love salt, feel free to add it to taste. Serve these with the Pickled Green Onions on page 34—a magical pairing.

SNACKS, FRITTERS, TARTS

Pepper Shrimp

WITH PICKLED GREEN ONIONS

For four

4 green onions, thinly
  sliced diagonally
1 Scotch bonnet,
  seeded and
  thinly sliced
4 garlic cloves,
  thinly sliced
4 tsp sweet smoked
  paprika
¼ cup/60ml white wine
  vinegar
¼ cup/60ml olive oil
12¼ oz/350g raw,
  shelled, and de-
  veined large shrimp
Lime wedges and
  Pickled Green
  Onions (page 34),
  to serve

First, place the green onions, Scotch bonnet, and garlic in a mixing bowl. Add the paprika, vinegar, olive oil, and shrimp, mix well, and refrigerate for 30 minutes to marinate. Don't marinate the shrimp any longer, otherwise you run the risk of them going rubbery.

Heat a skillet or frying pan on medium–high heat, then add the shrimp and pan fry them for 4–5 minutes, turning occasionally, until they just turn pink and are cooked through. Serve with lime wedges for squeezing over and pickled green onions on the side.

Alternative: if you want to make these shrimp with the shells on, make the marinade without the vinegar and marinate the shrimp overnight. Then, about 30 minutes before cooking, add the vinegar and mix well. (Don't forget to de-vein the shrimp, if they haven't already been de-veined.) Cook as described above.

Sweet, nutty, and delicious, cassavas are more filling and nutritious than potatoes, or so I've heard. These, along with Honey Jerk Wings (see page 73), have seen me through some of my longest days. After a hard shift in the kitchen, nothing hits quite like them—especially the ridiculously crispy scraps that have chipped off other fries. I live for them. They can stand side by side with big and bold flavors, like Spiced Ketchup (see page 43), or Hot Pepper Sauce (see page 40) mixed into mayo, for those who are partial.

You can make the fries immediately after you've steamed the cassava, but I prefer to prepare them in big batches up to that point and then freeze them. I then fry them from frozen and they come out fluffy with a beautifully crisp outside.

SNACKS, FRITTERS, TARTS

Fluffy Cassava Fries

For two

1 cassava (about
   8 inches/20cm long)
Sunflower oil,
   for deep-frying
Fine sea salt and
   ground black pepper

Peel the cassava, making sure that you remove all the skin, including any red flesh, so that only white flesh remains. Cut your cassava into thirds, then halve each third lengthwise. Remove the core—a fibrous root that runs down the middle of the cassava and is usually visible. If you miss it, once the cassava has been steamed, the core is very noticeable and you can remove it then. Cut the cassava into fry-sized pieces—about ½ inch/1cm thick and about 2 inches/5cm long.

In batches, place the cassava fries in a steamer basket and steam until you can pierce the flesh with a sharp knife without any resistance—this should take about 15 minutes (but can be longer if your pieces are bigger). Make sure the cassava isn't overcooked as the fries will shred and start to fall apart. Using tongs (they'll be hot), carefully remove the cooked pieces and set them aside to cool while you cook the remaining batches. Allow the fries to steam dry for 5–10 minutes before frying. The cassava is ready to fry once it's tacky to the touch. (Or, at this stage you can freeze the cassava in portions, frying from frozen another time.)

Half-fill a deep, wide saucepan with sunflower oil. Once the oil is hot (about 356°F/180°C on a cooking thermometer; or use the wooden-spoon test on page 244), fry the cassava fries in batches, taking care not to overcrowd the pan, for 2–3 minutes, turning with a slotted spoon, until light golden brown all over. Drain the cooked fries in a bowl lined with paper towels to drain, and continue frying until all the fries are cooked. Season with salt and pepper to serve.

These may have started life as a vegan version of My Saltfish Fritters (see page 63), but they have standing of their own and allow for the green onions, Scotch bonnet, and spices to dial up the flavor in tasty harmony with sweet pumpkin. Whereas the saltfish fritters have a doughy texture, these are crisp—you get an ASMR moment as you bite into a crunchy outer shell that gives way to a gently doughy inner. They make a perfect vessel for Ginger Chile Sauce (see page 43). You can swap out the pumpkin for butternut squash or even plantain, if you prefer—although if you have a waterier squash, be mindful to add less extra water to the batter.

SNACKS, FRITTERS, TARTS

Pumpkin Fritters

For four
(12–16 fritters)

1 cup plus 3 tbsp/150g
  all-purpose flour
1¾ tsp baking powder
1 tbsp thyme leaves
  or 1 tsp dried thyme
½ tsp Top Spice Mix
  (page 23)
2¼ tsp Jamaican Curry
  Powder (page 24)
¼ tsp ground cumin
¼ tsp ground coriander
½ tsp ground black
  pepper, plus extra
  to season if necessary
½ tsp fine sea salt,
  plus extra to season
  if necessary
¼ Scotch bonnet,
  seeded and
  finely chopped
2–3 green onions,
  thinly sliced, to taste
1 cup/225g pumpkin
  or butternut squash
  flesh, grated
¾ cups plus 2 tbsp/
  200ml water
Sunflower oil,
  for deep-frying

Pop the flour, baking powder, and the herbs, spices, and dry seasonings in a mixing bowl and stir to combine. Mix in the Scotch bonnet, green onions, and grated pumpkin or squash, then gradually add the water little by little, mixing well each time, until you have a batter that reluctantly drops off the spoon (you don't want it too runny).

To deep-fry, heat about a 4-inch/10cm depth of sunflower oil in a wide, deep saucepan. To shallow fry, heat about 2 inches/5cm of oil in a medium frying pan. Either way, make sure the oil doesn't come more than halfway up the side of the pan. When it's hot, drop in a small spoonful of the batter—if it sizzles when it hits the oil, the oil is ready. Taste test the cooked batter to check for seasoning, adjusting if necessary.

Using two large spoons (one to scoop and one to scrape off the batter into the oil), fry your fritters in batches of about four to six at a time for 2–3 minutes each side, until golden and crispy. Set each batch aside to drain on paper towels, while you fry the remainder. Serve hot with your sauce of choice.

These bites are incredibly light and fresh. They came to be when I was trying to create my own version of "shark and bake," a fast-food beach snack popular in Trinidad and Tobago. As it goes, the event nearly broke me—I didn't sleep for the best part of 48 hours, cooking three courses for over seventy people, and making every single thing from scratch. But, by the time my eye stopped twitching and the balmy summer breeze blew through our hidden gem of a venue, it all seemed worth it. I couldn't find shark easily in London and, for environmental reasons, nor was I keen on trying. So, I settled on hake. Although it's not as meaty as shark, it is a worthy alternative—and its slightly sweet flavor helped me showcase Green Seasoning (see page 36). These bites are great as a snack, and even better lovingly stuffed into a Coco Bread Bun (see page 182) with Plantain Chips (see page 57) and Spiced Ketchup (see page 43), which is how I served them at that supper club.

SNACKS, FRITTERS, TARTS

"Shark" Hake Bites

WITH LIME & GREEN SEASONING

For four to six

14 oz/400g skinless
    hake fillets (or other
    sustainable white fish)
Pinch of fine sea salt,
    plus extra for salting
Sunflower oil,
    for deep-frying
1½ cups/200g all-
    purpose flour
½ tsp ground turmeric
¼ tsp ground white
    pepper
1 tsp baking powder
½ tsp dried mixed herbs
½ tsp garlic powder
2 egg whites (whisked
    until foamy) or
    7 tbsp/100ml
    sparkling water
6 tbsp/90ml Green
    Seasoning (page 36)
Lime wedges,
    for squeezing
A few cilantro leaves
    (optional), to garnish

Place the fish fillets in a baking dish and sprinkle generously with salt. Let them rest for 30 minutes to firm up, then rinse and pat them dry with a clean kitchen towel or paper towel. Cut the fish into strips about ¾ inch/2cm wide.

Half-fill a deep, wide saucepan with sunflower oil and place it on medium–high heat. The oil is ready for frying when it reaches 356°F/180°C on a cooking thermometer (or use the wooden-spoon test on page 244).

While the oil is coming to temperature, in a medium bowl mix together 1 cup plus 2 tbsp/150g of the flour with the turmeric, white pepper, baking powder, mixed herbs, garlic powder and pinch of salt. Put the remaining 6 tbsp/50g of flour into a separate bowl, and the foamy egg whites or sparkling water into a third. Add the green seasoning to the foamy egg whites or water and give them a whisk or two to combine.

A few strips at a time, dip your hake pieces first in the plain flour, then in the egg/water mixture, then coat them in the spiced flour. Fry for 2–3 minutes, turning, until your batter is nice and golden all over and the fish is cooked through. Remove the fried strips with a slotted spoon and set them aside to drain on a plate or in a colander lined with paper towels. Repeat until all the strips are cooked. Squeeze with a little lime, then serve scattered with cilantro, if you wish.

When I eat these wings, I leave the bones clean, which, as those who know me will tell you, is something I rarely do. The wings will not disappoint if you cook them in the oven, but when you can, cook them outside over fire to enjoy that authentic smokiness. My friend Melissa Thompson, one of the best live-fire cooks I've had the pleasure of knowing, uses bay leaves and soaked pimento berries to cook any jerk, giving a greater depth of flavor. In Jamaica, the locality enables barbecuing over pimento wood; in the UK and the US, soaked berries and leaves honor that tradition. The honey jerk glaze, followed by salt and pepper sprinkled on as soon as you have finished cooking the wings, is the finisher to end all finishers.

SNACKS, FRITTERS, TARTS

Honey Jerk Wings

For four

1 lb 2 oz/500g chicken
   wings
1 tsp Top Spice Mix
   (page 23)
½ tsp fine sea salt
1 tsp ground black
   pepper, plus extra
   to season
4 tbsp/60ml Jerk
   Marinade (page 28),
   plus extra if needed
2 tbsp olive oil
1 tbsp honey, plus
   extra if needed
Sea salt flakes

Place the wings in a mixing bowl and add the spice mix, salt, and pepper. Massage everything into the skin and even underneath it if you can. Add 2 tablespoons of the marinade and massage again. Cover the bowl and place it in the fridge, letting the chicken marinate for at least 6 hours, but ideally overnight. About 30 minutes before you intend to cook, remove the wings from the fridge to bring them up to room temperature. Preheat your oven to 425°F.

Transfer the wings to a medium roasting pan and cook them for about 10 minutes, or until you start to see the chicken skin getting a little crispy. Turn your oven down to 375°F and cook for 20 minutes, until the wings are starting to take on some color.

Meanwhile, make a glaze by mixing together the olive oil with the remaining 2 tablespoons of the jerk marinade and the honey, adjusting the mixture with more marinade and/or honey, according to taste. Set aside.

Take the wings out of the oven and brush the glaze over the skin. Increase the heat to 425°F and return the wings to the oven for 15 minutes, until they are sticky and have started blackening and are cooked through.

Meanwhile, combine equal amounts of sea salt flakes and ground black pepper in a small bowl. As soon as you remove the cooked wings from the oven, use your fingers to immediately crush and scatter the seasoning over the top. Serve straight away.

Quick to make and incredibly irresistible, this is a vegan alternative to my Pepper Shrimp on page 64, and a star in its own right. The sauce is stickier here, so that it clings to the crunchy tofu. Add it to a bowl of rice to turn it into a meal; and it's so good with the Pickled Green Onions (page 34) or the Pickled Chow Chow (page 39).

SNACKS, FRITTERS, TARTS

Peppered Tofu

For four

7 oz/200g firm tofu, drained
¾ cup/80g cornstarch
1½ tsp fine sea salt
2 tbsp sweet paprika
Sunflower oil, for deep-frying
3 tbsp white wine vinegar
3 tbsp olive oil
1 tbsp light or dark brown sugar
2 tbsp water
1 Scotch bonnet, seeded and thinly sliced
4 garlic cloves, thinly sliced
3 green onions, thinly sliced

First, drain the tofu (to ensure maximum crispiness). Wrap it in a clean kitchen towel or in paper towels. Place it on a large plate or chopping board, then place another chopping board on top. Pop something heavy on top of that—I use two or three cookbooks, but bags of flour or a few cans will do. Let press for 20–30 minutes.

Reserve ½ tablespoon of the cornstarch, then tip the remainder into a mixing bowl. Add the salt and half the paprika to the bowl and mix. Set aside.

Half-fill a medium–large frying pan with oil and place it on medium–high heat. Cut your drained tofu into roughly ¾-inch/2cm cubes, place the cubes in the bowl with the flour mixture, and stir to coat. Dust off the excess and add a test cube to the hot oil—if it bubbles, you're good to go.

Turn the heat down to medium and fry the cubes in batches, turning, for 3–4 minutes, until crisp all over. Remove each batch with a slotted spoon and set the pieces aside on a plate lined with paper towels, to drain the excess oil. Repeat until all the pieces are cooked, topping up the oil and bringing it back to frying temperature as needed.

While your tofu is cooking, in a small bowl, mix the vinegar, olive oil, reserved ½ tablespoon of cornstarch, remaining paprika, and the sugar and water and whisk to combine. Set aside.

Once you have finished frying the tofu, remove all but 1 tablespoon of the oil from the frying pan. Place the pan back on medium heat and add the Scotch bonnet, garlic, and green onions. Cook for 1 minute, then add your whisked sauce. Cook until the sauce is honey-like in consistency and the garlic and onions are softening. Add the fried tofu back into the pan and stir to coat and warm through. Serve immediately.

This unassuming (on account of its few ingredients), but no-less-great Cuban snack is a perfectly crisp fritter with the most tender of centers. You needn't worry if you think the fritters seem to be lacking in the spice department—the treat is in the malanga's own creamy texture and the fact that, for something deep-fried, the fritters are so light and so deeply irresistible. Parsley adds a fresh, herby note, with the garlic coming through sweetly. Dip them into Mojo Sauce (see page 31) that has been cooked for an extra 5–10 minutes to deepen and soften the garlic flavor.

Also known as cocoyams, malangas are hairy like cassavas, but without wax applied to the skin. The flesh is slippery, so I usually use a kitchen towel to hold the root while grating. Malanga is commonly interchanged with eddoe or taro—all starchy roots from the Araceae family that look similar. Feel free to swap as availability dictates.

SNACKS, FRITTERS, TARTS

Malanga Fritters

For four to six
(12–16 fritters)

½ tsp Top Spice Mix
    (page 23)
2 garlic cloves, grated
⅓ cup/10g flat-leaf
    parsley, leaves
    and stems finely
    chopped, plus
    optional extra
    to serve
1 tsp fine sea salt
1 egg, beaten, or
    ½ tbsp all-purpose
    flour
1 lb/450g malanga,
    peeled, grated, and
    rinsed
Sunflower oil,
    for deep-frying
Sea salt flakes
    (optional),
    for sprinkling

Put the spice mix, garlic, parsley, salt and egg or flour in a mixing bowl and whisk to combine. Add the grated malanga and mix well. Cover the bowl and place the mixture in the fridge to chill (transfer it to an airtight container if you want to chill it for a couple of days before cooking).

When you're ready to cook, half-fill a large frying pan with oil and place it on medium–high heat. Once the oil is hot (about 356°F/180°C on a cooking thermometer; or use the wooden-spoon test on page 244), take a large spoonful of the mixture and use a second spoon to slide it into the pan. Repeat for another three fritters, frying four fritters at a time, so that the pan isn't too busy.

Cook each batch for 3–4 minutes, flipping halfway through, until golden brown all over and nice and crisp (they should still be soft and tender on the inside). Remove each batch with a slotted spoon or spatula and place the fritters on a baking sheet lined with paper towels to drain any excess oil. Repeat until you've cooked all of your fritters, then sprinkle them with sea salt flakes and the extra chopped parsley to serve, if you like.

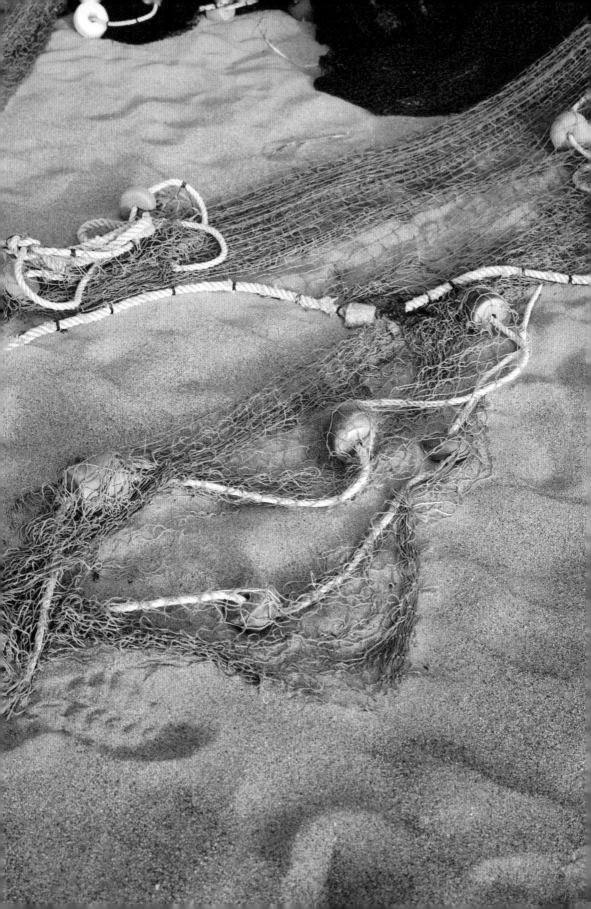

Meat, Poultry, Fish.

In the Caribbean, we like our flavors bold, and there's
no better way to add depth and complexity of flavor
to your food, with what feels like minimal effort, than
through marination. I love a good marination, not least
because good things come to those who wait, and
giving dishes time to let the spices do their thing
before cooking will only ever reward your patience.
I'm a forward-planner. I grew up in a household where
peas were left soaking for hours, and chopped onions
and garlic, along with the contents of the huge spice
drawer in our kitchen, were smeared over chicken before
being put away to marinate in the fridge overnight.
So—the mindset to start preparing my food hours
in advance comes naturally to me. If it's not something
you're used to doing, I implore you to give it a go,
the end result will be so much the more special for it.

Every dish in this chapter can be cooked in several
ways—barbecue, broiler, or oven. Each method has its
own pull; I don't vote any better than the others.
That said, if you have a drum or barbecue, the smell
of good foods wafting their spices up and around creates
a sort of heady excitement that reminds me so much
of warmth and sunshine, and that smoky flavor
is what they like to say is *chef's kiss*.

Fried fish reminds me of my nan. I'd say it's one of her signature dishes. Popping in to see her for a "quick" chat with my mum on a Saturday would mean leaving with a little hard dough, a plantain, and a foil with some fried fish. Mum would always say Nan should save it for herself, and Nan would always quip she had plenty. It was sweet exchange, a dance that would mean Mum went away with breakfast for the following day.

Escovitch is a lightly cooked pickle that the Spanish introduced to Jamaica. The vegetables soften as a result of the cooking, rather than by sitting in the vinegar. Pop it on top of the fish only once you're ready to serve—you don't want the fish to soften underneath those punchy vegetables.

MEAT, POULTRY, FISH

Fried Fish Escovitch

For two to four

1 tsp onion powder
½ tsp ground pimento
½ tsp garlic powder
1 tsp ground white
  pepper
½ tsp fine sea salt,
  or to taste
7 tbsp/100ml sunflower
  oil
2 whole sea bass
  (about 1¾ lb/800g
  each), gutted and
  scaled

For the escovitch
1 small onion
½ red bell pepper,
  seeded
½ yellow bell pepper,
  seeded
¼ Scotch bonnet
  (optional), seeded
1 small carrot, peeled
  and julienned
1 tbsp water
1 tsp dark brown sugar,
  plus extra if needed
3 tbsp red wine vinegar

Mix together the onion powder, pimento, garlic powder, white pepper, and salt in a small bowl and set aside. Then give your fish a little rinse (I always like to do this when serving it whole, whether I've gutted it myself or not, as it removes any lingering scales). Grab your seasoning bowl and rub three-quarters of the mixture on the skin of your sea bass and the remaining one-quarter equally inside each cavity. Set aside, ready for frying.

Heat the sunflower oil in a large frying pan (big enough to fit your whole fish) on medium–high heat. If you don't have a frying pan large enough, cut the fish in half. When hot, place the first fish into the pan, and turn down the heat to medium. Fry the fish for 5–6 minutes on each side, until cooked through and the skin is crispy. Remove and set aside. Repeat for the other fish, then set the fish aside and keep them warm on serving plates.

Make the escovitch: Thinly slice the onion, both bell peppers, and the Scotch bonnet (if using). Drain the oil, leaving behind 2 tablespoons in the pan. Add your thinly sliced vegetables, including the carrot, and the water. Add the sugar and cook for 2 minutes on medium–high heat, until the liquid has reduced by around half. Add your vinegar, then taste. If the sauce is too tart, add a touch more sugar. Turn the heat down to medium, simmer for 3 minutes, then serve over the fish.

I long to be in my mother's presence again, if only for a minute to hold her hand. This recipe, which I've done my best to re-create, is that hand hold. It's the squeeze of reassurance that brings comfort; the reminder I ache for most days. Food and memory sit side by side like firm friends, and B's Roasted Chicken transports me to many places, but none more than Mum's last dining table. We would sit and chat—sometimes aimlessly, sometimes about the important stuff—for hours. At times we would eat this roasted chicken alongside Pops' Mac Pie (see page 126); at others it would be the centerpiece of a Sunday roast, but on a Tuesday. Who says roasts are solely for a Sunday? Cook this often, abandoning the rules. When you do, I hope you feel the hug I feel. It's the endless warmth of B.

MEAT, POULTRY, FISH

B's Roasted Chicken

For two to four

1 lb 2 oz/500g skin-on, bone-in chicken thighs

1 small onion, finely chopped

3–4 garlic cloves, finely chopped

2 tsp Top Spice Mix (page 23)

2 tsp mixed herbs

1 tsp dark soy sauce (low sodium is fine)

2 tbsp olive oil

Prepare the thighs either first thing in the morning on the day you intend to serve, or (ideally) the night before. Put all the ingredients into a mixing bowl. Massage everything into the chicken, including under the skin, then cover the bowl and put the thighs in the fridge to marinate overnight, if possible.

About 30 minutes before you intend to cook, remove the thighs from the fridge to bring them up to room temperature. Line an ovenproof dish with foil (enough to be able to wrap the chicken like a parcel), and preheat your oven to 400°F.

Transfer the thighs to the dish and wrap the foil around them, scrunching the opening to seal. Place the dish in the oven and cook the thighs for about 50 minutes, by which time they should have started to brown. Open the foil parcel and cook for 10 minutes, until the meat is cooked, tender, and juicy, with a light, crisp skin.

Mountain "Chicken," as it's known in Dominica and Montserrat, is actually the giant ditch frog, but since this species is now endangered, I'm using frog legs from an unprotected species. You can dispense with the frog legs altogether, though, if you like, and use chicken wings, but the flavor is slightly different. Frog legs are more a combination of chicken and crab, in my opinion. They're also lower in fat, so more delicate—be careful not to overcook them or they'll be rubbery (145°F/63°C on a cooking thermometer, if you have one, is perfect). Mountain chicken is traditionally served with ground provisions, but I love it with Pops' Mac Pie (see page 126).

MEAT, POULTRY, FISH

Mountain "Chicken"

For four to six

¼–⅓ cup/60–80ml lime juice (about 2 limes)
2 tbsp white wine vinegar
2 lb 2 oz/1kg frog legs or chicken wings
4 garlic cloves, minced
1 tsp fine sea salt
2 tsp thyme leaves, plus a couple of sprigs for the sauce
½ tsp ground white pepper
½ tsp Hot Pepper Sauce (page 40)
About ½ cup plus 1 tbsp/70g all-purpose flour
Sunflower oil, for frying
2 tbsp olive oil
2 tbsp unsalted butter
1 onion, diced

Mix the lime juice and 1 tablespoon of the vinegar in a small mixing bowl. Add the frog legs or chicken wings and mix to coat well. Drain away the excess liquid and set aside.

In a separate bowl, mix together the garlic, salt, thyme, white pepper, pepper sauce, and remaining 1 tablespoon of vinegar. Add this to the bowl with the meat and massage in the marinade. Cover the bowl and place it in the fridge for about 3 hours (but not more than 4 hours).

About 30 minutes before cooking, bring the meat up to room temperature. Then, tip the flour onto a baking sheet and dredge the legs or wings through it just before you fry.

For frog legs, heat about ⅔ cup/160ml of sunflower oil in a large frying pan; for chicken wings, use 1 quart/1 liter of oil in a deep saucepan (not more than half full). Heat on medium–high heat until it reaches about 356°F/180°C on a cooking thermometer (or use the wooden-spoon test on page 244). In batches, fry the legs or wings, making sure you don't overcrowd the pan. The frog legs should take 3–4 minutes, turning, until golden all over; the chicken wings, 8–10 minutes. Using a slotted spoon, remove each batch to a plate or colander lined with paper towels. Keep warm in a very low oven while you fry the remainder.

Once you've finished cooking the meat, heat the olive oil and butter in medium frying pan on medium heat until the butter has melted. Add the onion and the thyme sprigs and cook for 5–7 minutes, until the onion has softened. Turn the heat down and cook until it starts to take on a little color (1–2 minutes should do it). Remove from the heat and drizzle the buttery onions over the legs or wings to serve.

The Caribbean is known for being a tropical paradise, with an ocean that brings with it an abundance of fish and seafood. Fish can handle strong flavors like those of this lovely marinade. Don't be tempted to swap ground coriander for fresh cilantro—I find that ground has softer, more floral notes, which complement this dish. If you're short on time, the Green Seasoning (if you have some prepared) on page 36 works well instead—you'll want to add the oil, lemon, and salt and pepper on top, though, pouring off any of the liquid. If you can't find swordfish, substitute any local, sustainable meaty fish instead. Grilled swordfish is great for barbecues, but if the weather is a little drearier, bring the barbecue energy indoors. The sweet spiciness of the Mango Chow on page 110 is a good match for this herby preparation.

MEAT, POULTRY, FISH

Griddled Swordfish

For four

3 garlic cloves, peeled
½ large shallot or
    1 small shallot,
    peeled and roughly
    chopped
1 green onion,
    roughly chopped
¼ tsp thyme leaves
½ tsp ground coriander
2 tsp lemon juice
    (about ½ lemon)
2 tbsp olive oil
4 swordfish steaks
    (about 8 oz/220g
    each)
Fine sea salt and
    ground black pepper

Blitz all the ingredients except your swordfish steaks in a food processor, until you have a smooth marinade.

Pat the fish dry and put it in a dish (preferably a glass one) big enough to hold all the steaks in a single layer. Season your fish with salt and pepper and pour the marinade over the top. Turn the steaks over so that both sides are evenly coated. Let them marinate at room temperature for 15 minutes.

You can broil, barbecue, or griddle the steaks, according to your preference (if you're using a griddle pan, make sure you brush it with a little oil first, so that the steaks don't stick). Whichever method you choose, you'll need medium–high heat and the steaks will need 3–5 minutes each side, depending on size—you want the outside of the steaks to be browned with a little pink left inside.

This is a fairly hands-off dish (the marinating and chilling do most of the work), but it tastes like something that you've labored over for days. If you have the time, a long marination is close-your-eyes-and-imagine-yourself-eating-it good! I once left it for three days and the result was sensational. Also, marinating the meat uncovered allows for the skin to dry out, which means crispy crackling.

Spanish flavors dominate Cuban cuisine. In this case, the citrus tenderizes the meat while allowing the other notes to penetrate. If you're not a garlic fan, I'm sorry . . . this recipe might not be for you. Serve it on a bed of Moros y Cristianos (see page 118) with more Mojo Sauce (see page 31), and maybe the Malanga Fritters (see page 76) to start.

MEAT, POULTRY, FISH

Mojo Roasted Pork

For four

4 garlic cloves, peeled
½ tsp fine sea salt
14 black peppercorns
1 small shallot, finely diced
¼ tsp dried oregano
1 tbsp olive oil
½ cup/120ml Mojo Sauce (page 31)
2 lb 2 oz/1kg skin-on, boneless pork shoulder
A few fresh oregano leaves, to garnish

In a mortar or mini-processor, grind the garlic, salt, peppercorns, shallot, oregano, and oil to a paste. Set aside.

If your pork has come with its skin intact, carefully slice it away from the meat, leaving the end attached, so that you can open it out like a book. Place the pork in a roasting pan and, with the skin flapped open, use a skewer to poke the meat all over, without piercing all the way through. Pour your mojo sauce over the meat, then rub in the garlic marinade. Fold the skin over and transfer the joint to the fridge, uncovered, to marinate for at least 24 hours.

About 30 minutes to 1 hour before cooking, take the pork out of the fridge to come up to room temperature. Preheat your oven to 400°F. Rub a sheet of foil with a little oil and then wrap it, oiled side downward, over the pork, sealing at the edges of the pan.

Place the pork in the oven and immediately lower the heat to 350°F. Cook for 2 hours, then remove the foil and lift the skin to baste the flesh (keep the skin as dry as possible). Roast the pork for 1 hour, until cooked—it should start to feel as if it'll fall apart when you shred it with a fork. Remove the pan from the oven, turn the oven up to 425°F, then remove the foil and pour the sauce from the pan into a bowl (set this aside). Cook the pork, uncovered, for a further 30–40 minutes, until you have crispy crackling. Keep an eye that it doesn't burn. Let rest for 30 minutes, then shred the meat using two forks, to serve with the reserved juices poured over the top—they are too good to waste! Serve sprinkled with oregano leaves.

I made these at a Windrush event in the early days of Island Social Club. That day, we played dominoes and told journey stories, mapping the routes and legacies that brought our families and friends to the "Motherland." It was a quieter affair than some of our other events, for reasons that lean into the conscious forgetfulness of the contribution that Caribbeans have made to the West; it was an honoring of the hardships our parents and grandparents had undergone in the UK. During the 1980s and '90s, there had been a gradual erosion of the spaces in which Black British communities could come together in this way, which meant moments like those at this gathering were all the more poignant.

When you cook these burgers, you can skip the honey and glaze them with extra sauce at the end of cooking; or dispense with both and use the Ginger Chile Sauce (see page 43) instead. I love them with Fluffy Cassava Fries (see page 66).

MEAT, POULTRY, FISH

Jerk Lamb Burgers

For four

2 shallots, very
  finely diced
2 garlic cloves,
  finely diced
2–3 tbsp Jerk Sauce
  (page 29)
½ tsp fine sea salt
¾ tsp ground black
  pepper
Pinch of grated nutmeg
¾ tsp ground pimento
¾ tsp ground
  cinnamon
1 tsp garlic powder
1 tsp onion powder
¼ tsp ground coriander
1 lb 2 oz/500g lean
  ground lamb
Sunflower oil,
  for brushing

For the glaze
1 tbsp Jerk Sauce
  (page 29)
1 tsp honey

Place all the ingredients except the oil and those for the glaze in a bowl and mix everything together with your hands (use more or less of the jerk sauce, according to your heat preference). Divide the mixture into four equal portions and shape each portion into a ball. Then, flatten each ball into a burger shape, aiming to keep the burgers as even in thickness as possible—aim for ½–¾ inch/1–2cm thick for each one.

Brush a griddle pan with a little oil and heat it until hot. Cook the burgers two at a time (if your griddle is big enough) on high heat, until they're cooked to your preference. I like 4–5 minutes each side. (They will need about the same amount of time under a hot broiler or on a barbecue.)

For the glaze, combine the jerk sauce and honey in a small bowl. Brush the glaze on the top of your burgers, then flip them onto the glazed side for a few seconds, so that the tops get a little sticky before serving.

Mumma, bless you for making these ribs. These were one of my earliest tastes of indulgence. Mum would often serve them with either sautéed potatoes (heaven), Hard Dough Bread (see page 172), or leftover boiled dumplings that she would then fry (see page 181). My, oh my—I cannot tell you how delicious they were with the gravy she would make from the remains of the sauce. For someone who hated cooking, she was good at it (except for timings . . . never her forte). These were one of her standout dishes. I'm re-creating the ribs from my memory, so I've likely taken a few liberties, but I suppose that makes them my own. Were she here, she would no doubt offer me some constructive criticism, but overall I think she'd be pretty happy with the changes, and the results. A top meal from a top Mumma.

MEAT, POULTRY, FISH

Sticky BBQ Ribs

For four

2 lb 2 oz/1kg pork spare ribs or baby back ribs
4 tsp mixed dried herbs
1 tbsp Top Spice Mix (page 23)
½ cup/135g ketchup (I use my spiced one on page 43)
¼ cup/60ml dark soy sauce
1 tbsp ground black pepper
¼ cup/60ml honey
2 tbsp white wine vinegar

Place the ribs in a deep roasting pan. In a bowl, mix together the remaining ingredients to make a marinade. Spoon the marinade over the ribs and massage it in, then cover the roasting pan with foil and let the ribs marinate in the fridge overnight.

When you're getting ready to cook, take the ribs out of the fridge for 30 minutes to 1 hour to bring them up to room temperature. Preheat your oven to 400°F.

Bake the ribs for about 3 hours for spare ribs and 2 hours for baby backs, turning them halfway through cooking and basting with the sauce in the pan, until they are tender, but not falling off the bone. (If you want to finish off the ribs on a barbecue, rather than in the oven, get the barbecue ready while the ribs are baking.)

Remove the foil and either finish off the ribs in the oven for 15–20 minutes or on the medium–hot barbecue. The result will be ribs that are nice and sticky.

Known as the "nature island of the Caribbean," Dominica is a place I long to visit. Mostly covered in rainforest, it also has hot springs, volcanoes, and rare flora and fauna. I know all that from spending far too long on Google lusting at photos, but its spirit I know from the stories I've heard from friends whose mums were born there. Dominica has the largest community of Caribs, now known as the Kalinago people, in the region. These are the survivors of colonialism—first came the French (the Spanish deemed the place "too hard to control"), whose influence is still evident in the island's food and place names, and then came the British, whose cultural hangover lingers. The surviving peoples are, I think, what give the island its majesty.

You might think there's a lot going on in this recipe, but the mango chutney and rum glaze make it exactly the kind of food that gets me excited. I prefer to use fresh ginger and garlic and molasses sugar, as they create richness, but you can easily swap in fresh for ground spices and use brown sugar. This is so good wrapped in a roti (see page 175), with Sweet Tangy Coleslaw (see page 112) and a touch of yogurt.

MEAT, POULTRY, FISH

Reef Chicken

For four

8 skin-on, bone-in
   chicken thighs
1 tsp fine sea salt
½ tsp ground black
   pepper
Packed ¼ cup/50g
   molasses sugar or
   dark brown sugar
4 tbsp/60ml dark rum
2 tbsp/30ml lime juice
2 tsp white pepper
¾ oz/25g ginger root,
   grated, or 1 tsp
   ground ginger
1 tsp ground cloves
½ tsp ground
   cinnamon
¼ lemon, finely grated
   zest only
1 garlic clove, grated
3 tbsp Mango Chutney
   (page 32)
Flat-leaf parsley, leaves
   roughly chopped,
   to serve (optional)

Place the chicken in a large bowl and massage the salt and black pepper into and under the skin. Set aside.

In a mortar, mix together the molasses or brown sugar and 2 tablespoons of the rum, along with the lime juice, white pepper, ginger, cloves, cinnamon, lemon zest, and garlic, pounding a little to make a paste. Massage this into the chicken, including under the skin, then cover the bowl and refrigerate for at least 1 hour, but no longer than 24 hours.

About 30 minutes before you intend to cook, remove the meat from the fridge to bring it up to room temperature and preheat the oven to 400°F. Place the chicken, skin side up, in a shallow baking pan and bake it for 45 minutes, or until the juices run clear.

Meanwhile, in a bowl whisk together the mango chutney with the remaining rum until combined.

Baste the skin of the cooked chicken with the rum-laced chutney, then return it to the oven for 3–4 minutes, until the chutney is warm. Or, if you want extra-crispy skin, heat your broiler to high and place the glazed chicken under the broiler, leaving it until the skin starts to caramelize. Serve sprinkled with roughly chopped parsley, if you wish.

We migrate.

I rarely let myself think about the way that my ancestors departed Africa for the Caribbean. My imagining of it is indescribably, inescapably painful—but it happened. I think of the journeys across the ocean. The individuals whose bodies were claimed by the waves. The loss of life, the loss of family, the loss of identity. Without this history that weighs heavily on our shoulders, who would we be?

My nan often insists that "we don't come from slaves"— as though the creamy skin and straight hair of my Syrian great-great-grandmother negated the other lines of ancestry that have flowed into our blood. I've never challenged this statement. Nan will soon be ninety, and she grew up in a time when the grip of colonial colorist attitudes was even tighter throughout the Caribbean than it is today. I'm aware of my privilege in being able to look at such statements with compassion, to think critically and to engage in understanding who I am and where I come from—a freedom not often gifted to our grandparents and parents. Survival rarely allows time for critical thought.

Our complex history comes from our displacement, as does the richness of our culture. Not richness in the sense of capitalist wealth, but in the deep rooting of our souls. I am not naïve—a more equitable distribution of land and money would make for less strife and strain, and I can only hope that what was taken will eventually find its way back. The people who were trafficked to the Caribbean on board slave ships, and later arrived after the abolition of slavery through indenture schemes—their displacement bred ingenuity, their creativity forged strength and beauty. Suffering was prevalent; broken spirits were not. Resilience has for so long been part of our being that it can at times feel like some people believe it to be the sum of our parts, meanwhile overlooking our softer, gentler qualities. Even so, the Western values that were forced upon the displaced people disrupted their cultural practices.

A movement toward reclaiming lost traditions is gaining traction now, not just within the African communities but within other cultures that were ripped apart by empire and colonialism, too. Although we can never re-create immigrant existence in a space outside of the white lens, we can imagine what an authentic life might have been like. By moving away from extreme forms of capitalism and centering ourselves in community, we can prioritize rest and joy. Pain has so long been at the core of our identity that prioritizing peace has become a radical act, ushering in a new wave of cultural reclamation.

When I got married, in 2019, I felt the need to hold on to my last name—it had been central to my identity for thirty-three years. However, the ancestry test I took two years later revealed the tenuousness of my Scottish heritage, harking instead back to the darkest part of my existence. The suspicions I'd grown up with were confirmed, presented as data on a computer screen. And yet I keep my name with a reflective pride. Once it felt vital to my identity, now it helps me to understand my past. This name is all I've ever known, and its erasure won't scrub the history of how it, and I, came to be.

My parents moved to London as wide-eyed eight-year-olds. It was a confusing experience for them—from the sunshine of the Caribbean to the grim high rises and grody housing that passed for accommodation in the "mother country." Their welcome was lukewarm at best, downright hostile at worst. The food was gray and bland, lacking in spice and color. The education they received was sub-par—Dad recalls the boredom of classes at least two years behind his age group in the Caribbean. I'm reminded of conversations I've had and am still having with friends; tales of tediousness being explained away by teachers as stupidity, funnelling bright young Black children toward exclusion or expulsion. Mum consumed information—she was an avid reader, always with at least three books on the go. They would both have thrived in higher education. But as Windrush children, and the eldest in their families, this wasn't a course they were encouraged to pursue. For a long time, I didn't understand why my parents were so passionate about our schooling—my brother more obviously academic, me a lot more subtly so—but they made sure that we were "well" educated. These days I cringe at the thought of how little I cared about education.

The enforced movement of millions of chained Africans to the Caribbean and the Americas—the so-called "middle passage"—caused seismic shifts on both sides of the Atlantic. More recently, what the historian Sir Hilary Beckles has called the "Windrush middle passage" has further disconnected us from our continent of origin, reinforcing the lack of cohesion within our already fragmented culture. Still, to be a second-generation immigrant, born and raised in the UK, is to have hope, even if things are still far from equal. We continue to strive for justice—in my case, quietly . . . rebellion isn't always about the fight, it can also be about peace, to offer grace with a kindness you may not always have experienced; to resist shame and embrace joy without guilt.

So how do we move toward a post-colonial world? Ownership. This is *our* history, and it falls to us to acknowledge it happened. In the UK, the authorities have missed countless opportunities to apologize for past atrocities, while the exclusion of our history from the school curriculum smacks of erasure. Collectively, we urgently need reparative justice. Many people balk at the idea of reparations—but the notion jut isn't as simple as financial redress. It's a commitment to invest in infrastructures that were knowingly neglected and to work toward the redistribution of extracted wealth. Too often I hear it said that British leaders should not have to apologize for the past, that we should all just move on. But why? In the past lies in our present: this history is now.

You might be wondering what all this has to do with a cookbook. I can confidently say: everything. Food is political, but it's also history, and one of the purest expressions of it. So many of our food legacies aren't written, they're passed from generation to generation, a physical story without words, in the form of movement.

Sides, Provisions, Rice.

The recipes in this chapter are those that I took totally for granted when I was growing up—the ground provisions that Mum bought each week, which I would only move around my plate. (Aside, perhaps, from the sweeter plantain and yam that I would happily eat.) I didn't appreciate their value—neither their flavor, nor their role as the linchpins of our Sunday roast, let alone the importance of the role their preparation played in the life of our family, and of our ancestors. But I savor them now, as they've taken on meaning with the passing of time. Once, I would have described these dishes as sides, but really, they deserve more recognition, for without them the more complex dishes would be incomplete. They're all part of a bigger picture, and to exclude them would be to leave blank spaces.

Elsewhere in this chapter, you'll find recipes to bring freshness to your plate. The tang of some lightly dressed fruit or vegetables, or the creaminess of a little avocado pear—these side dishes will enhance a rich, complex curry, stew, or fried fish, and balance the palate. And then there's the rice and the mac pie, without which no Caribbean feast would be complete.

These salad dressings are bold in flavor in a way that is typical of the cuisine. Sweet-and-sour dressings, like both of these, offer a freshness that balances with richly flavored curries and stews, or partners with spicy dishes for a little relief from the heat. You can easily scale the quantities up or down in the following two recipes, and they also keep well in the freezer. Just make sure you give them a good whisk when you defrost them, as they'll separate during the freezing process.

SIDES, PROVISIONS, RICE

Pineapple & Lime Dressing

½ pineapple, peeled, cored, and blended

6 tbsp/90ml extra-virgin olive oil

¼ cup/60ml white wine vinegar

4 tsp lime juice (about ½ lime), plus extra if needed

Fine sea salt and ground white pepper

Strain the pineapple pulp through a sieve and then tip into a food processor along with the oil, vinegar, and lime juice. Blitz until smooth. Season to taste with salt and pepper, and more lime juice, if needed.

Serve drizzled over the Ackee and Saltfish Tarts (see page 54) or over an accompanying salad. The dressing will last for a couple of days in an airtight jar in the fridge (or you can freeze it; see above).

Sweet & Sour Dressing

2 tbsp white wine vinegar

2½ tbsp lime juice (about 1 lime)

¼ cup/60ml extra-virgin olive oil

2 tbsp honey, plus extra to taste if needed

Fine sea salt and ground black pepper

Pop all your ingredients in a jar, give them a good whisk with a fork, and season with salt and pepper to taste. Check for flavor and add a little extra honey if you feel it's too tart. The dressing will last for a couple of days in an airtight jar in the fridge (or you can freeze it; see above).

I love how those from Trinidad and Tobago consider chow a snack. It's delicious, but fiery as it is with Scotch bonnet, it is definitely not for the faint-hearted. Many Caribbeans are exposed to chile pepper from a young age, and, personally, I love it. If you're not great with chile, though, feel free to include less or none. I proudly sniff as I devour this.

Mango Chow

For four

6 garlic cloves, peeled
2 large shallots, halved
1–2 Scotch bonnets
(to taste), seeded
2 green mangoes,
peeled, pitted
¼ cup/10g cilantro,
stemmed
½ tsp fine sea salt,
plus extra to taste
¼ tsp ground black
pepper, plus extra
to taste
2½ tbsp lemon or lime
juice (about 1 lemon
or lime)
1 tsp white wine
vinegar

Thinly slice the garlic cloves, shallots, Scotch bonnets, and mangoes, and roughly chop or tear the cilantro.

Place these and all the remaining ingredients in a bowl and mix well with a spoon. Taste and adjust the salt and pepper and citrus juice to your preference.

You can serve the chow immediately, but it's best left to rest in the fridge for at least 1 hour first for the flavors to develop.

Order Caribbean take-out, whatever the meal, and you'll get coleslaw on the side. It's normally creamy with mayonnaise, and occasionally includes something fruity. Frankly, it's never been for me—I want to love it, and I've tried, but I'm just not a fan of mayo. Coleslaw serves a purpose: it gives a cooling refresh, while you eat all the other rich and layered dishes. Fresh, juicy, and tangy, this version is pretty much the only coleslaw I ever serve and can ever be seen munching—usually at the end of a busy event or service. Cabbages vary hugely in size, so feel free to up the dressing quantity, if you need.

SIDES, PROVISIONS, RICE

Sweet Tangy Coleslaw

For four

¼ small red cabbage
¼ small white cabbage
1 red onion
1 large or 2 medium
  carrots
½ quantity of Sweet
  and Sour Dressing
  (page 109)
Fine sea salt and
  ground black pepper

Finely shred both cabbages, thinly slice the onion, and peel and julienne the carrot.

Put them all in a mixing bowl and give them a good toss to evenly distribute the vegetables, then give your dressing a good shake or a whisk with a fork (it will separate while resting) and add it to the coleslaw. Give everything a good mix and make sure all your vegetables are coated. Season with salt and pepper to taste, then serve.

I make this salsa for the sole purpose of showing off the avocado pear. Caribbean avocado, or "pear" as it's known there, has either bright green or purply black skin and is so creamy you can use it instead of butter. In the seventeenth century, it's said that it was eaten sweet with a little wine or lemon, and sugar. Just as I do now, Mum would put expertly cut slices on hard dough bread and eat them just like that. Another thing: it makes the most delicious milkshakes (as I discovered on my travels). This salsa is a nod to all the histories of this humble "pear."

SIDES, PROVISIONS, RICE

Avocado Pear Salsa

For four

9 oz/250g cherry
  tomatoes, halved
2 green onions,
  thinly sliced
2½ tbsp lime juice
  (about 1 lime)
4 tsp white wine
  vinegar
1 tsp light brown sugar
1 avocado pear
Fine sea salt and
  ground black pepper

Put the tomatoes and green onions into a small mixing bowl. Set aside.

In a separate small bowl, whisk the lime juice, vinegar, and sugar until the sugar has dissolved. Then, add this to the bowl with your tomatoes and green onions. Toss with the dressing, and season with salt and pepper to taste.

Halve the avocado pear, remove the pit and, with the flesh still cupped in the skin, slice the flesh into cubes, each a similar size to the tomato halves. Scoop these out of the skin with a spoon, straight into the bowl. Mix well and serve.

Richie, my brother, would always ask Mum and Dad to cook extra rice and peas for him to take back to college to freeze. He probably felt the same way about making the dish as I did—why bother when your parents do it so well? My dad soaking the peas on a Saturday night and the smell of them cooking on Sunday morning was a weekly ritual in my house. Now, it's a vivid memory—of my mum with her headscarf on, and my dad, stirring bubbling beans on the stove, occasionally taking one out to squeeze it and see if it's cooked.

Various versions of this dish exist, each with its own story, but all firmly tying back to West African *waakye* roots. My immediate family has always used aduki beans (that are smaller than the more common kidney beans), so that's what I use, too.

SIDES, PROVISIONS, RICE

Home Rice & Peas

For four

¾ cup/150g dried aduki beans, soaked overnight in water, or 1 x 15-oz/425g can of aduki beans
3 green onions, finely chopped
1 onion, finely diced
3 garlic cloves, peeled and smashed
5 thyme sprigs
1 tsp dried mixed herbs
1 tsp fine sea salt
1 Scotch bonnet
1½ cups/300g white basmati or long-grain rice, rinsed
¾ cup plus 2 tbsp/ 200ml full-fat coconut milk

If you're using soaked dried beans, drain them and tip them into a saucepan with 3⅓ cups/800ml of water. Add the green onions, onion, garlic cloves, thyme sprigs, dried mixed herbs, and salt to this pan. Place the pan on medium–high heat and bring the liquid to a boil. Then, lower the heat and simmer until the beans are almost cooked—about 40 minutes to 1 hour. If you're using canned beans, just add them to the saucepan with their canning liquid, 2½ cups/600ml of water and the green onions, onion, garlic, thyme, dried mixed herbs, and salt (there's no need to cook them).

Gently pierce the Scotch bonnet once with the tip of a knife, then add it to the pan with the aduki beans, along with the rice and coconut milk. Stir. (You don't have to pierce the chile, but if you don't, keep an eye on it and remove it before it bursts, as you're looking for it to bring flavor, not heat.)

Put the lid on the pan and cook until the rice is tender, and the liquid has evaporated—this should take 20–25 minutes. Remove the pan from the heat and let the rice and peas rest, untouched with the lid on, for 10 minutes. After 10 minutes, remove the lid and use a fork to fluff up the rice, ready to serve.

Moros y Cristianos is a Cuban cousin of rice and peas (see page 117), which, in English, translates as Moors and Christians. The name is a reference to the Reconquista, a seven-centuries-long struggle on the Iberian peninsula between the Islamic Moors (represented by the beans) and various Christian kingdoms (the rice). What I have yet to unearth, though, is how a dish so close to *waakye* rice and peas came to represent a series of military campaigns ending around the same time Christopher Columbus "discovered" Cuba. The transatlantic slave trade began around this time, too, so perhaps the dish found its way to Cuba through the movement of Africans; or perhaps it was in fact the influence of the Moors, the collective term for the medieval Muslim populations of North Africa and parts of southern Europe who moved around, trading commodities wherever they went. All I know is that I was very pleased to see what I had thought to be rice and peas when I sat down in a government restaurant in Cuba, hungry and excited for a little home comfort. The flavor was much subtler, with the sofrito doing the work rather than the creaminess of coconut milk. I prefer it without the traditional bacon, but if you want to include this, fry it until crisp, then set aside, using the bacon fat to cook the sofrito. Then, fold the meat back in at the end of cooking.

SIDES, PROVISIONS, RICE

Moros y Cristianos

For four

1 tbsp olive oil
1 onion, finely diced
½ large green bell
  pepper, seeded
  and finely diced
½ large red bell
  pepper, seeded
  and finely diced
2 garlic cloves,
  chopped
1 cup/200g long-grain
  white rice
1 tsp ground cumin
1 tsp dried oregano
1 bay leaf
½ tsp fine sea salt
1 x 15-oz/425g can of
  black beans
¾ cup plus 2 tbsp/
  200ml water

Heat the olive oil in a heavy-bottomed medium pot on medium heat. Add the onion and both bell peppers and cook for about 5 minutes, until they are starting to soften. Add the garlic and cook for no more than 1 minute—keep an eye, you don't want anything to color. Add all the remaining ingredients, including the water in the can of beans, and stir. Bring the liquid to a boil, then turn down the heat to a simmer and cook for about 20 minutes, until the rice has absorbed most of the liquid.

Then, place the lid on the pot and cook the rice for 15 minutes, until all the liquid has evaporated. Turn the heat off and let rest (with the lid on) for 10 minutes. Remove the lid and fluff up the rice with a fork before serving.

Ground provisions, provisions, or the colloquial term "hard food" are catch-alls for certain fruits and vegetables that Caribbeans often serve in or alongside soups or stews or with meat and fish. Among them are cassava, dasheen (taro), sweet potato (red skinned with white or yellow flesh), yam, plantain, breadfruit, green banana, malanga, and eddoe.

Hard foods are rich in vitamins and minerals, often more so than their Western counterparts and, although not all are native to the islands, those that made their way through trade from Africa, Asia, and Oceania found the perfect climate to grow in abundance, providing plentiful, cheap, and satisfying food. At home in London, we would often have them with our Sunday roast.

SIDES, PROVISIONS, RICE

Boiled Provisions

For four to six (roughly)

1–2 tsp fine sea salt, to taste
1 small–medium yam, peeled and cut into 1-inch/2.5cm chunks
2 green bananas, peeled and cut into thirds, or skin rinsed and halved
2 small sweet potatoes, peeled and cut into 1-inch/2.5cm chunks
2 yellow plantains, peeled and halved, or just rinsed and halved

In a deep, wide saucepan, bring enough water to a boil to cover the vegetables. Add the salt, yam chunks, and green bananas first. Then, after about 5 minutes, add your remaining vegetables and cook until they will slide off a sharp fork easily. This will normally take 20–30 minutes, depending on the vegetables.

If at any point some vegetables are ready earlier than others, simply remove them with a slotted spoon and set them aside. If you're cooking your plantains and green bananas in the skin, drain them and allow them to cool a little before peeling. Serve the veg with meat, fish, or Ital Coconut Stew (see page 147), or with the ackee and saltfish filling on page 54. Alternatively, you can let them cool and fry them—see page 122.

I like a little hard food (see page 120), but I love a little fried hard food. When I'm in the Caribbean, I am particularly partial to fried breadfruit. It's pretty much the sexiest potato chip you ever had, but bigger and goes well with hot dishes, and won't disintegrate or become soggy.

You're unlikely to boil and then fry the plantain, as frying without boiling yields similar results, as seen on page 58, and boiled plantain is delicious on its own—but you can, and I have. For cassava, see the fries on page 66, but again you can fry it once you've boiled it, too. If you have any leftover Boiled Provisions, this is the perfect way to use them up.

SIDES, PROVISIONS, RICE

Fried Provisions

For four to six
(roughly)

1–2 tsp fine sea salt,
  to taste
1 small–medium yam,
  peeled and cut into
  1-inch/2.5cm chunks
2 green bananas,
  peeled and cut into
  thirds, or skin rinsed
  and cut in half
2 small sweet potatoes,
  peeled and cut into
  1-inch/2.5cm chunks
2 yellow plantains,
  peeled, or just rinsed
  and halved
Sunflower oil, for frying
Fine sea salt

First, boil and drain your hard food according to the method on page 120.

Once you have drained all the hard food, let them cool and pat them dry. Then, cut them into smaller slices—just shy of ¼ inch/5mm should do it. (If you're cooking from leftovers, they can be quite slippery, so you may need to wash your hands in between handling each of them.)

Half-fill a medium frying pan with oil and heat it on medium–high heat. Once the oil is hot (about 356°F/180°C on a cooking thermometer; or use the wooden-spoon test on page 244), fry the vegetables in batches, taking care not to overcrowd the pan, for about 2 minutes each side, until slightly colored—they won't turn as brown as you might think, but they'll harden. If they're starting to burn, turn the heat down a little. Pick or scoop out the cooked vegetables with a fork or slotted spoon, setting them aside on a plate or colander lined with paper towels.

Once you've cooked all the vegetables, give them a taste, and, if needed, add a little salt. (Remember, they have first been cooked in salted water, so you might not need any extra salt.) Serve immediately.

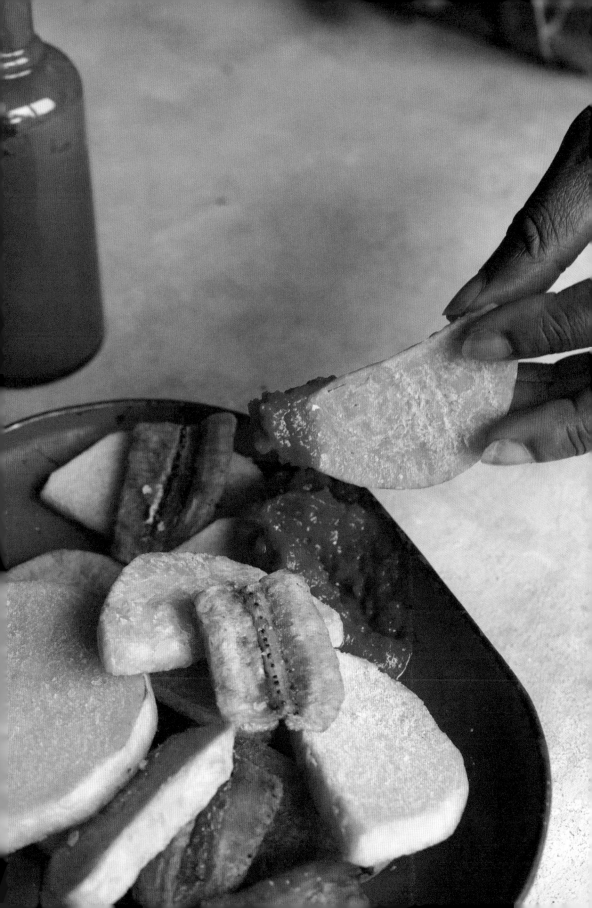

Here is a hands-off way to prepare plantain that is lighter than frying (see page 58) but adds more depth than boiling (see page 120). It is very good alongside a stew, particularly when it's the Low, Slow Oxtail Stew on page 164, or as a dessert—sprinkled with a little cinnamon and served with rum cream (see page 210) or drizzled with salted caramel and served with Stout Punch Ice Cream (see page 209).

SIDES, PROVISIONS, RICE

Whole Baked Plantain

WITH SALT OR CINNAMON

For four

2 yellow plantains
Sunflower oil,
   for brushing
   and drizzling
Sea salt (for savory)
   or ground cinnamon
   (for sweet), to
   sprinkle

Preheat the oven to 400°F. Line a baking sheet with parchment paper and coat it with some sunflower oil.

If you're roasting your plantains in their skins, give them a rinse and scrub them with a vegetable brush. Pierce a couple of holes along each plantain, as if you were baking a potato. If you want to roast the plantains without their skins, cut down one of the seams on each plantain and peel the skin away.

Place the plantains on the baking sheet. If you've peeled them, drizzle with a little oil and rub it around the plantains before sprinkling them with a little salt for a savory finish or cinnamon for a sweet one—or try a little of both! Bake the plantains for about 30 minutes, turning them halfway through cooking, until tender and golden, or until a knife can pierce into the flesh without resistance.

Pops, as I began calling my dad in my early twenties (probably to annoy him), is famed in South London for his macaroni pie . . . mostly among our friends and family, but famed nonetheless. In the Caribbean, macaroni and cheese is much more pie-like, made with eggs rather than white sauce. Once the pie sets, cutting squares of cheesy pasta is a comfort, which is almost certainly the reason why I consumed so much of it while pregnant and in the early days of parenthood. While I sat (trapped) on the same corner of the sofa feeding a tiny baby who could not be sated, it's what Pops brought over to help; and the dish I had so often requested to have with Mum's roasted chicken (see page 89). This dish is a reference to my dad; his influence on me and my cooking, and how his mac pie has held me in times of joy and of pain. I took some liberties when creating my version, but it is a chance to honor a man who continues to guide many, whose kindness and generosity is centered around food, and without whom I would not be writing this today.

SIDES, PROVISIONS, RICE

Pops' Mac Pie

For six

1 lb 2 oz/500g macaroni
3 tbsp unsalted butter
2 eggs, beaten
1 tbsp tomato paste
¾ cup plus 2 tbsp/
    200ml whole milk
14 oz/400g strong, hard
    cheese (I like aged
    cheddar), grated
¼ cup/8g flat-leaf
    parsley, stems
    removed and leaves
    finely chopped, plus
    extra for sprinkling
½ tsp Top Spice Mix
    (page 23)
1 tsp ground black
    pepper, plus extra
    for sprinkling
2 tsp Ginger Chile
    Sauce or Hot Pepper
    Sauce (page 43 or 40)
Fine sea salt

Preheat your oven to 375°F.

Cook the macaroni in boiling salted water for 6 minutes, or until it's al dente. Drain it in a colander, tip it back into the pan, and stir in the butter until melted.

While the macaroni is boiling, combine the beaten eggs, tomato paste, milk, and three-quarters of the cheese in a bowl. Once you've stirred the butter into the macaroni, add the egg mixture to the pan, mixing until well combined. Then, add the parsley, spice mix, pepper, and ginger chile or pepper sauce and mix again. Season with salt to taste.

Transfer the macaroni to an ovenproof dish, one that will nicely nestle the pie to 1½–2 inches/4–5cm deep. Sprinkle the remaining cheese on top, along with a little extra black pepper and parsley. Bake the pie for 30–40 minutes, or until it is firm and golden. Remove the dish from the oven and let the pie cool and set for 10–20 minutes before cutting and serving.

Curries, Soups, Stews.

I'm known for my curries, and I'm known for my love of a Dutch oven. Aside from the (rather dull) fact that cooking in one pot makes the clean-up easier, it also means you get to create dishes where ingredients are nestled with one another, slowly transforming to become a dance of flavors. One of my favorite things is to throw—masterfully, I like to think—a bunch of things into a pot, hopefully ending up with something steaming, rich, and fragrant. No dish is ever quite the same twice, of course, but over time the iterations will evolve into something distinctively your own.

Many of the cross-currents that have influenced Caribbean cuisine are most strongly felt in these dishes: stews from the original indigenous inhabitants harnessing the richness of cassareep, as seen in My Pepperpot (see page 160); curries by way of the Indian indentured laborers who brought their knowledge of more complex spicing to the Caribbean. There's a special primal joy in cooking these recipes, as they replicate practices passed down through the generations, cementing their importance within Caribbean culture.

I fell in love with Cuba. It proved to be a place where I could step back in time, switch off, and both observe and immerse myself in the culture. We were invited into people's homes, and reminded what generosity looks like. It was humbling.

This popular Cuban soup, with its regional variations across the island and traditionally featuring ham hock, is often served thick on a bed of white rice. I have omitted the meat in my recipe, choosing instead to keep it vegan. Using canned black beans makes it speedy, too—I love a long-labored cook, but sometimes I want things on the table quickly. The result is comforting and wholesome; I feel like I'm righting the wrongs of the world when I eat it. At home, I forgo the sugar, but I've left the sugar in as an option, in case you prefer your soup sweeter.

CURRIES, SOUPS, STEWS

Black Bean Soup

For six

2 tbsp olive oil
2 small red onions,
    plus extra to garnish
1 red bell pepper,
    seeded
1 green bell pepper,
    seeded, plus
    extra to garnish
5 garlic cloves,
    finely chopped
½ tbsp dried oregano
½ tbsp ground cumin
½ tsp ground black
    pepper
2 x 15-oz/425g can of
    black beans, drained
½ tsp fine sea salt
2 tbsp balsamic or
    apple cider vinegar
1¼ cups/300ml
    vegetable stock
    or water
2 bay leaves
Pinch of smoked
    paprika (optional)
½ tsp light brown
    sugar (optional)

Finely dice the red onions and the red and green bell peppers. Heat your olive oil in a Dutch oven on medium heat. When hot, add the onions and both bell peppers and cook for 5–7 minutes, until they start to soften. Add the garlic, oregano, cumin, and black pepper and cook for 1 minute.

Add the drained beans to the pan with the salt, vinegar, stock or water, and bay leaves. If you're keen to add a little smoked flavor, add the pinch of smoked paprika, and the sugar if you would like a touch of sweetness. Cook with the lid on for 20 minutes, for the flavors to meld.

Take the pot off the heat. If you want a thicker soup, using an immersion blender, blitz until half the beans are pureed (leave the soup as it is, if not). Garnish with finely chopped red onion or green bell peppers (or a combination of both), and serve straight up, or more traditionally on top of a bed of cooked white rice.

In 2019, Island Social Club opened in London for a year-long restaurant residency, and this was one of the curries we had on the menu. I derive so much pleasure from cooking it, and it's the one I have spent the most time trying to perfect. I've learned that not all coconut milk is created equal, and a watery one can throw the entire curry off; but the toasted rice in the Colombo Curry Powder really helps to thicken that sauce—it's a must.

Colombo made its way to the French-speaking Caribbean islands from Sri Lanka. In many Caribbean curries, the potent yellow color comes solely from the ground turmeric, but here provenance introduces yellow mustard seeds. Caribbean history is mapped within our food . . . in this case, Sri Lanka to India, India to the Caribbean, the Caribbean to a small kitchen in East London—all reminding me of how we are so deeply interconnected, so tethered to one another, no matter how often we try only to highlight our differences. Maybe that's why this might just be my favorite curry.

CURRIES, SOUPS, STEWS

Chicken Colombo

For four

1 lb 5 oz/600g skinless, boneless chicken thighs, halved
½ tsp fine sea salt, plus extra to season
¾ tsp Top Spice Mix (page 23)
2 tbsp Colombo Curry Powder (page 24)
1 tbsp sunflower oil
1 tbsp coconut oil, plus extra if needed
3 large shallots, peeled and sliced lengthwise
½ oz/15g ginger root, peeled and finely chopped

Place the chicken thighs in a medium mixing bowl and add the salt, spice mix, and curry powder. Massage the mixture into the flesh, then cover the bowl and let the chicken marinate in the fridge for at least 4 hours, but preferably overnight.

Remove the chicken from the fridge 30 minutes before you intend to cook, to come up to room temperature. Place a medium pot on medium–high heat. Add the sunflower oil and fry your chicken in batches for 1–2 minutes on each side (you can do this in a frying pan, if it's easier), removing each batch from the pot and setting it aside on a plate while you brown the remainder. Deglaze your pan with a little water and dry it out (take care, as it'll be hot). I always pour the deglazing liquid into a bowl and taste it; if it's not bitter, I save it for the stock.

Add the coconut oil to the pan and let it heat up on medium heat. When hot, add the shallots and allow them to sweat for 5 minutes, until they're softening but not coloring (keep

3 garlic cloves,
  finely chopped
¼ Scotch bonnet,
  seeded and
  finely chopped
1¼ cups/300ml chicken
  stock
1½ cups/360ml full-fat
  coconut milk (at least
  60% coconut content)
8½ oz/240g pumpkin
  or butternut squash
  flesh, diced into
  1-inch/2.5cm chunks
1 chow chow, peeled
  and diced into
  1-inch/2.5cm chunks

an eye on them as they can burn quickly—add a little more coconut oil if you need to). Add the ginger, garlic, and Scotch bonnet and cook for 1–2 minutes, stirring occasionally, until you start to smell the warm aromas. Add your stock, coconut milk, and pumpkin or squash, then let the veg cook for 10 minutes, before returning your chicken to the pot, tucking in the pieces so they're just submerged. It'll feel like there might not be enough liquid, but you only want the chicken to be just covered.

Poach the chicken for 10 minutes, then add the chow chow, and season with salt to taste. Put the lid on the pot and cook, covered, for about 30 minutes, or until the squash and chow chow are softened and the chicken is cooked through. Chicken thighs can still look a little pink when poached, so it's best to check with a thermometer if you have one (the internal temperature should read 167°F/75°C). If not, make sure the juices are running clear.

When I recollect the eating choices of my youth, I see a pattern of accidental conformity. We ate the foods of my heritage softly, as though a secret, never to be shared outside of family or close friends. Curry goat (or mutton) is rich and unctuous and my tendency for accidental conformity has meant that I found my way from big pots of it bubbling at community halls and served on flimsy plates, to spice and steam hitting my face as I opened take-out polystyrene containers, to serving a boneless version in my own restaurant. For a time, I didn't understand the importance of serving something as it was meant to be served—without worry, honoring its origins and free from the need to amend or soften a dish to make it suitable for those not accustomed to its ways. Cooking curry goat now, in the way of this recipe, feels like a true celebration of those who came before, who were moved from many lands and, with limited options, created gold. I've stopped conforming to other people's palates. This recipe is as it should be, and it is priceless in its ability to comfort.

CURRIES, SOUPS, STEWS

Curry Goat (or Mutton)

For four

1¾ lb/800g bone-in goat or mutton shoulder, cut into bite-sized pieces
1 tbsp fine sea salt, plus extra to season
2 tbsp Jamaican Curry Powder (page 24)
1 tsp ground black pepper
2 tbsp sunflower oil, plus extra if needed
3 onions, peeled and finely chopped
8 garlic cloves, finely chopped
1 oz/30g ginger root, finely chopped
1 Scotch bonnet, seeded and finely chopped
3⅓ cups/800ml water
10 thyme sprigs
7 oz/200g waxy potatoes, diced into ¾-inch/2cm cubes

Tip the meat into a large mixing bowl and add the salt. Really massage it in, as this will tenderize the meat to result in a melt-in-your-mouth curry. Add your curry powder and black pepper and massage these in, too. Cover the bowl and let the meat marinate at least overnight, but ideally for up to 72 hours—at which point time will have really worked its magic.

On the day you intend to make the curry, remove the meat from the fridge 30 minutes to 1 hour before cooking to come up to room temperature.

Heat 1 tablespoon of the oil in a wide frying pan on medium–high heat. Add the meat in batches, leaving plenty of space in the pan, turning it for 1–2 minutes, until the pieces have browned on each side, sealing in your spices. Set aside each batch on a plate, while you brown the remainder. Add more oil as needed.

Meanwhile, heat the remaining 1 tablespoon of oil in a deep, wide saucepan on medium heat. When hot, add the onions, put the lid on the pan, and let them sweat for 7–10 minutes, until well softened. Check on them from time to time, and, if they look like they are burning, add more oil. Remove the lid to add your garlic, ginger, and Scotch bonnet, then stir and pop your lid back on for 2–3 minutes, until everything in the pan is soft.

Tip your meat back into the saucepan. Add the water, or enough to make sure you're just covering the meat, the thyme sprigs, and a pinch of salt and give the contents of the pan a good stir.

Turn the heat up to bring the curry to a rolling boil, then lower the heat to a simmer. Pop the lid on and let the curry cook, checking it every 30 minutes or so to stir and stop it from sticking to the pan, for 1½–2 hours. Add the potatoes and check the seasoning, adding a little more salt if needed. Cook for 30 minutes, or until the potatoes are cooked and the meat is tender enough to split with a wooden spoon without much pressure. Serve the curry on a bed of steamed white rice or Home Rice & Peas (see page 117).

The tradition of Saturday soup is believed to have originated with the Taínos. They would keep a pot of slow-cooking vegetables and fish or meat, yielding a hearty soup. I'm not using meat, so my take on it is quicker, but as with all Caribbean food, don't rush. Let the flavors develop, before thickening and finishing with the Spinners (see page 178). If you prefer a non-vegan version, though, you can easily incorporate meat if you wish—adding some Mitchell Curry Chicken (see page 163) would work well. Poach the chicken in the broth for 20 minutes before incorporating the vegetables.

CURRIES, SOUPS, STEWS

Saturday Soup

For four

4 garlic cloves, peeled
2 small onions, peeled
¼ Scotch bonnet
1 celery stalk
¾ oz/20g ginger root, peeled
2 tbsp sunflower oil
1 tsp Jamaican Curry Powder (page 24)
2 tsp ground coriander
2 carrots, peeled and diced
7 oz/200g new potatoes, peeled and diced
1 red bell pepper, seeded and chopped
1 yellow plantain, peeled and cut into ½-inch/1cm coins
2 cups/480ml vegetable stock
2 bay leaves
3 tbsp coconut cream
1 quantity of Spinner dough (page 178)
1 corn-on-the-cob, shucked, or ⅔ cup/100g frozen corn
Fine sea salt and ground black pepper

Put the garlic, onions, Scotch bonnet, celery stalk, and half the ginger in a food processor and pulse until minced. Finely chop the remaining ginger with a sharp knife. Set aside.

Heat the oil in a large, wide saucepan on medium heat. When hot, add the processed ingredients, frying for 1–2 minutes to release the aromas. Add your curry powder and ground coriander, cook for 1 minute, then pour in a little more oil if anything starts to stick.

Tip in the carrots, new potatoes, red bell pepper, and finely chopped ginger and fry for another 1 minute. Then, add the plantain, stock, bay leaves, and coconut cream. Bring the liquid to a simmer and cook like this for 10 minutes, while you ball and roll your spinners (see page 178).

Once the 10 minutes are up, gently drop your dumplings into the pot, along with the shucked corn kernels or frozen corn. Place the lid on the pan and cook for 15 minutes, or until the dumplings are floating and the plantain is cooked (you should be able to pierce the slices easily with a sharp knife).

Ital is a food-based tenet of Rastafarianism, rooted in Jamaican resistance to globalization and the honoring of the Maroons, runaway Africans who founded free communities during Jamaica's occupation. Ital's consistent themes are having a deep respect for the land and not consuming processed foods. It is a spiritual practice, animated by the concept of Livity; an essential life energy that flows from produce to person. Connection to the land through the time-honored practice of intercropping—an agricultural technique passed on from the Maroons—and through an Ital diet supports the earth and those who farm it. This is a simple Ital curry that highlights the vibrational energy of good produce. Use the best ingredients you can find.

CURRIES, SOUPS, STEWS

Ital Chickpea Curry

For four

3 tbsp sunflower oil
1 onion, thinly sliced
2 large shallots, thinly
    sliced
½ tsp ground turmeric
    or 1½ tsp finely
    chopped turmeric
    root
½ tsp Garam Masala
    (page 23)
½ tsp ground cumin
½ tsp Jamaican Curry
    Powder (page 24)
¼ tsp ground black
    pepper
⅓ oz/10g ginger root,
    peeled and chopped
6 garlic cloves,
    finely chopped
¼ Scotch bonnet,
    seeded (optional)
2 tomatoes, diced
2 cups/480ml
    vegetable stock
2 yellow potatoes,
    cut into ¾-inch/2cm
    cubes
2 carrots, diced
1 x 15-oz/425g can of
    chickpeas, drained
Fine sea salt

Heat 2 tablespoons of the sunflower oil in a medium saucepan on medium–low heat. Once hot, add the onion and shallots and cook them for 4–5 minutes, until softened. Add your turmeric, garam masala, cumin, curry powder, black pepper, ginger, garlic, and Scotch bonnet (if using). Stir everything in, add the remaining 1 tablespoon of oil. Cook for 30 seconds, then fold in your tomatoes, fully coating them in the spices.

Add 1⅔ cups/400ml of the stock (reserve the remainder), and the potatoes and carrots, season to taste, then pop the lid on the pan. Bring the liquid to a boil, then lower the heat and simmer for 20–25 minutes, until your potatoes and carrots are just cooked. Check the curry from time to time, adding a little of the reserved stock if it's looking dry.

Once the vegetables are cooked, fold in the drained chickpeas and cook for 5 minutes to warm through. If your curry is still a little watery, remove some of the potatoes, a large spoonful at a time, and mash them before returning them to the pan and mixing them in. Keep removing and mashing until you almost reach your desired thickness. Then, turn up the heat and cook the curry for at least 5 minutes so that it can thicken up fully. Taste, and adjust the seasoning if needed before serving.

Leonard Howell, an early preacher of Rastafarianism, introduced the idea of a plant-based diet to the Rastafari community after observing the diets of Indian indentured laborers. My Ital stew is not raw—the strictest version of the diet—but it makes me feel good—the uncomplicated nature of the food leaves me smugly satisfied.

CURRIES, SOUPS, STEWS

Ital Coconut Stew

For six

14 oz/400g coconut butter, chopped
4 carrots, peeled and cut into ½-inch/1cm chunks
1 savoy cabbage, shredded
14 oz/400g skin-on pumpkin or butternut squash flesh, grated
2 yellow plantains, peeled and chopped into ¾-inch/2cm coins
2 onions, finely diced
1 sweet potato, peeled and chopped into ¾-inch/2cm chunks
1 tbsp dried mixed herbs
1 tsp ground pimento
½ oz/15g ginger root, finely chopped, plus extra finely diced to serve
1 tbsp Jerk Rub (page 27)
¼ Scotch bonnet, seeded and finely chopped
Fine sea salt

To serve
1 tbsp sunflower oil
1 small broccoli, sliced

Heat about ¾ cup plus 2 tbsp/200ml of water in a wide, lidded saucepan on medium heat. Once the water is bubbling away, add the coconut butter and let it dissolve. Then, add the carrots and cook them for 10 minutes. Add the cabbage and cook for 3–4 minutes, until it starts to wilt—just keep an eye on the pan to make sure the cabbage doesn't burn, adding a little water if it does. This all forms the base for the stew.

Add the grated pumpkin or squash, the plantains, onions, and sweet potato. Stir, then add another ¾ cup plus 2 tbsp/200ml of water, if needed (you don't want it to be saturated in water, you're just using the water to avoid burning) and the herbs, pimento, ginger, rub, and Scotch bonnet. Mix everything together and season with salt to taste.

Put the lid on the pan, decrease the heat to low, and cook for 30–40 minutes, keeping an eye and stirring from time to time, to make sure you don't burn the bottom of the stew, until the vegetables are tender. Turn off the heat and allow the stew to steam with the lid on while you cook the broccoli to serve.

For the broccoli, heat the oil in a large frying pan on medium heat. When it's hot, add the broccoli slices and fry them for 2–3 minutes on each side, until browned.

Serve the stew topped with the fried broccoli and a sprinkling of diced ginger.

Jerk is the perfect adjective for this recipe, with its rich, smoky, sticky sauce full of complexity and heat that grows with each mouthful. I'm not one for modern meat replacements, I prefer vegetables treated with the same love as slow-cooked meats, and thoughtfully seasoned. Here, the jerk marinade does all the thinking for you after you've done the initial prep work. Just give it time and then throw it between a Coco Bread Bun (see page 182).

CURRIES, SOUPS, STEWS

Jerk Jackfruit

For four

3 tbsp olive oil
4 red onions,
    thinly sliced
1 tsp fine sea salt
½–1 tbsp honey, to
    taste
1 x 14-oz/400g can of
    jackfruit in water,
    drained
3 tbsp Jerk Marinade
    or Jerk Sauce
    (page 28 or 29)
1 x 14-oz/400g can of
    whole, peeled plum
    tomatoes
¼ tsp ground black
    pepper
¾ cup plus 2 tbsp/
    200ml water
4 Coco Bread Buns
    (see page 182),
    to serve

Heat the oil in a Dutch oven on medium heat. When hot, add the onions and ¼ teaspoon of the salt and sweat the onions for about 20 minutes, until they get a little sticky but not quite caramelized. Once they are almost there, add your honey—more or less, according to your taste—and cook for 1–2 minutes, while it starts to cook off.

Stir in the drained jackfruit and the jerk marinade or sauce and stir to combine, then cook for another 1–2 minutes. Add the tomatoes, ground pepper, the remaining salt, and the water and give it all a really good stir to combine. Pop the lid on the pot and cook for 30 minutes, then remove the lid and simmer the jackfruit for another 30 minutes, adding a little more water to prevent it from burning, if necessary, until the sauce has thickened, the tomatoes have sweetened, and the jackfruit has softened so that you can shred it easily. Serve stuffed inside the buns.

In my imagination, I have a home with land, where I head outside daily to pick from a bounty of fruits and vegetables. In life, I seek out nature wherever I can—including in the plant pots on my windowsill in East London. Picking my ripe tomatoes feeds my yearning for a life rooted in the earth. Whether you grow your own or not, enjoy this curry when tomatoes are at their peak—it's sweeter for it. Out of season, swap fresh for canned tomatoes and give the curry a little longer on the stove.

CURRIES, SOUPS, STEWS

Creamy Tomato Curry

WITH COCONUT & ROASTED SQUASH

For four

1 lb 2 oz/500g
  seasonal squash
  flesh, cut into
  ¾-inch/2cm chunks
3 tbsp olive oil
2 garlic cloves
⅓ oz/10g ginger root
¼ oz/5g turmeric root
  (or use ½ tsp
  ground turmeric)
¼ Scotch bonnet,
  seeded (or use a
  whole one, pierced)
1 onion, chopped
1 celery stalk, chopped
2 carrots, peeled
  and diced
7 oz/200g cherry or
  large tomatoes,
  pierced a few times
  with a sharp knife
1½ tbsp Jamaican Curry
  Powder (page 24)
1 tsp ground coriander
½ tsp ground cumin
1 x 13.5-oz/400ml can
  of full-fat coconut milk
Fine sea salt and
  ground black pepper
1 lime, juiced
  (optional), to serve

Preheat the oven to 400°F.

Tip your squash into a roasting pan with 1 tablespoon of the oil. Add a good few pinches of salt and pepper to season, and toss together. Roast the squash for 25–30 minutes, until soft but not mushy or crispy—you're just aiming to deepen the flavor. Set aside.

Meanwhile, mince your garlic and ginger, and fresh turmeric (but not the ground) and quarter Scotch bonnet (but not the whole), if using, in a mini-food processor, or grind them in a mortar with the pestle. Set aside.

Heat another 1 tablespoon of the oil in a medium, wide pan on medium heat. When hot, add the onion and celery and sweat for 5–7 minutes, until softened. Add the carrots and cook for 1–2 minutes. Add the tomatoes and cook for 5–7 minutes, until they start to collapse. Then, add the last 1 tablespoon of olive oil, along with the curry powder, coriander, and cumin (and ground turmeric, if using) and the garlic, ginger, turmeric, and Scotch bonnet mixture. Mix well and cook for up to 1 minute, until your spices start to release their aromas. Season with salt and pepper to taste.

Pour in the coconut milk and, if you haven't used the quarter chile, add the whole, pierced Scotch bonnet. Stir, bring the liquid up to a gentle rolling boil, and cook until your spices are fully incorporated into the sauce and it's as thick as you'd like it—I aim for it to reduce by almost half. Taste—if you haven't cooked off your spices for long enough, they can feel a little grainy on your tongue, in which case cook for a little longer. Fold in your squash and let it soak up all the flavors in the pan for a few minutes. Season with a little lime juice to serve, if you like.

150

Someone at a supper club said this soup was the star of the show—in a menu that also featured My Pepperpot (see page 160), Buss Up Shut Roti (see page 175), and Stout Punch Ice Cream (see page 209). The empty bowls suggested others agreed. Soup gets a bad rep, often thought of as bland and boring. This soup is neither: it is velvety, with curried pumpkin seeds adding textural crunch. I return to this particular soup whenever I want to have warmth radiated from the inside out. To me, in London, it marks a change from summer to autumn and the start of colder weather. Whatever I can do to hold on to the feeling of sunshine, I'm reaching for it.

CURRIES, SOUPS, STEWS

Squash Soup

WITH CURRIED PUMPKIN SEEDS

For six

1 lb 9 oz/700g butternut squash or Caribbean pumpkin, seeds reserved, flesh roughly chopped
1–2 tbsp sunflower oil
1 tsp salt, plus extra to season
½ tsp Jamaican Curry Powder (page 24)
1 small onion, minced
2 garlic cloves, minced
¾ oz/20g ginger root, minced
¼ Scotch bonnet, seeded and minced
2 large shallots, minced
1 large carrot, peeled and chopped
1 celery stalk, chopped
2 cups/480ml vegetable stock
2 bay leaves
A few thyme sprigs
Up to 1 x 13.5-oz/ 400ml can of full-fat coconut milk
1 lime, juiced
Ground black pepper

Preheat the oven to 350°F. Rinse the squash or pumpkin seeds thoroughly to remove any stringy flesh. Pat them dry and place them in a small bowl with ½ tablespoon of the sunflower oil, ½ teaspoon of the salt, and all the curry powder. Mix with a spoon, then spread out the seeds in a single layer on a baking sheet. Bake them for 25–30 minutes, tossing them every 10 minutes, until toasted. Set aside.

While the seeds are roasting, heat 1 tablespoon of the remaining sunflower oil in a medium–large saucepan on medium heat. When hot, add the onion and fry for 5–7 minutes, until soft and translucent. Add your minced ingredients and fry for 1–2 minutes, then add your carrot, celery, and squash or pumpkin, adding the remaining oil, if they look like they're sticking. Cook for 2 minutes, then pour in the stock and add the remaining salt, along with the bay leaves and thyme sprigs. Bring the liquid to a boil, then lower the heat to a simmer. Pop the lid on the pan and simmer the vegetables for 20 minutes, until everything is tender.

Scoop out the bay leaves and thyme sprigs with a spoon and remove the pan from the heat. Using an immersion blender, blitz the soup until smooth. Add half of the coconut milk, stir, and if the soup needs loosening a little, gradually add the remaining half, until the soup is velvety thick (not too thin). Return the pan to the heat to warm through, if necessary, and season to taste with salt and pepper, and a little lime juice. Serve hot with Hard Dough Bread (see page 172) or bread of choice.

There's a moment every year when my CSA box starts inundating me with corn. It acts as my gentle reminder of the movement of the seasons, urging me to take stock of variety and abundance before winter moves in. I'm a lifelong corn fan and I think generally it's underused. Like me, my daughter *loves* it. Now that she's at the age of toddler fussiness, if I can use the things she loves to encourage her to engage with ingredients she's less enthusiastic about, like cilantro, I will. I wanted a soup that made corn the centerpiece, showcasing how well it can balance with other big flavors. This is a non-traditional chowder (no fish)—but it is fresh, hearty, and filling. And fragrant, with a couple of big handfuls of cilantro. It's exceptionally good with the Squash and Thyme Bread on page 186.

CURRIES, SOUPS, STEWS

Corn Chowder

WITH RED BELL PEPPER & CILANTRO

For six

1 tbsp sunflower oil
2 onions, thinly sliced
2 celery stalks, chopped
3 garlic cloves, minced
¼ Scotch bonnet, seeded and minced
1 large shallot, minced
1 tbsp Jamaican Curry Powder (page 24)
1 red bell pepper, deseeded and diced
2 small–medium potatoes, peeled and diced
1½ cups/80g cilantro, leaves and stalks separated and chopped
Scant 4 cups/500g frozen corn
1 quart/1 liter vegetable stock
1 x 13.5-oz/400ml can of coconut milk
4 tsp lime juice (about ½ lime)

Heat the sunflower oil in a large saucepan on medium heat. When hot, add the onions and celery and sweat them for 5–7 minutes, until softened. Fold in your garlic, Scotch bonnet, and shallot and cook for about 1 minute, until fragrant.

Pop in the curry powder, let it cook for 1 minute, then add your bell pepper, potatoes, cilantro stalks, and corn. Mix everything well, then add the stock and a good pinch of sea salt and ground black pepper to season, and bring the liquid to a boil. Lower the heat to a simmer, and cook for 15–20 minutes, until your potatoes and bell pepper are tender.

Take the pan off the heat and add the coconut milk, lime juice, and chopped cilantro leaves. Using an immersion blender or a potato masher, blitz the soup to a chunky consistency. Season to taste again, then return the pan to the heat to warm the soup through before serving.

I waited three long years to go back to one particular spot in Grenada just to have this soup. But much had changed in those years, and sadly Patrick, who had first made it for me, had passed away. I sampled other versions on the island, and they were nice—some with saltfish, some without—but none were quite like Patrick's. On reflection, though, I realized that, while Patrick's soup was indeed delicious, what had really made it so special was the fact that the last time I ate it I had just got married. I was with my partner, my in-laws, and my parents—my newly formed family. It would be the last holiday I would have with my mum—who, with my dad, was giddy at having found Patrick's "proper" home-cooked food. The warmth and pride Mum and Dad surrounded us with that night—an extension of their culture, of Patrick, and of their people—reverberated with such strength that it left me dreaming about that soup for three years.

CURRIES, SOUPS, STEWS

Callaloo Greens Soup

For four

2 tbsp olive oil
1 onion, thinly sliced
1 celery stalk,
    roughly chopped
2 garlic cloves, sliced
3 green onions, sliced
¼ oz/5g ginger root,
    peeled and diced
1 pimento pepper
    (cherry pepper) or
    ½ Romano pepper,
    seeded and roughly
    chopped
5¼ oz/150g pumpkin,
    peeled, seeded, and
    roughly chopped
1 lb/450g callaloo
    (dasheen leaves) or
    spinach leaves,
    roughly chopped
1 x 13.5-oz/400ml can
    of full-fat coconut milk
1 tsp ground black
    pepper
1 cup/240ml water
Fine sea salt

Heat the oil in a deep saucepan on medium heat. When hot, add your onion and celery and sweat them for 5 minutes to soften a little, then add the garlic, green onions, ginger, and pimento (or Romano) pepper and cook for 2 minutes more until everything is just softened. Add your pumpkin, callaloo or spinach leaves, the coconut milk, the black pepper, and water. Stir to combine.

Pop a lid on the pan and bring the liquid to a boil. Lower the heat, then simmer the soup for 15 minutes if you used spinach or 20–25 minutes if you used callaloo, or until the pumpkin is cooked through.

Remove the pan from the heat and use an immersion blender to blitz it until smooth. Season to taste, then return the soup to the heat for 5 minutes to warm through before serving.

I'm obsessed with eggplants and I firmly believe they don't come better than when they are salty and crispy, as they are here before you fold them into the curry. I had one of those revelatory moments for this curry. Previous versions had lacked a roundness. Then, in the dead of the night, waking me from my dreams, the solution came to me—dark chocolate. Much Caribbean cocoa has a complex sweetness, which marries with the earthy flavors of the veg and spices in this curry. Cook this as often as you can when tomatoes and eggplants are in season.

CURRIES, SOUPS, STEWS

Eggplant Curry

WITH DARK CHOCOLATE & LIME

For four
(generously)

3 eggplants, halved
   and cut into
   1-inch/2.5cm chunks
Sunflower oil, for frying
1 tbsp yellow mustard
   seeds
1½ oz/40g ginger root,
   peeled and finely
   chopped
1½ limes, finely grated
   zest only
2 onions, finely
   chopped
4 tsp Garam Masala
   (page 23)
2 tsp ground coriander
2 tsp ground turmeric
½ tsp dried chile flakes
1 x 13.5-oz/400ml can
   of full-fat coconut milk
6 tomatoes, quartered
1 oz/30g 70% dark
   chocolate, broken up
1 x 15-oz/425g can of
   chickpeas, drained
Fine sea salt

Place the eggplant chunks in a colander set over a bowl and sprinkle them generously with salt. Let rest for 30 minutes, for the eggplant to release its water.

Heat 1 tablespoon of sunflower oil in a heavy-bottomed saucepan on medium heat. When hot, add your mustard seeds, fry them for 1 minute, then add the ginger and lime zest. Fry for 1–2 minutes more, or until the mustard seeds start to pop, then immediately stir in the onions, adding a little extra oil if necessary, and cook for 5–7 minutes, until softened. Add the garam masala, coriander, turmeric, and chile flakes, and fry for 1–2 minutes, then pour in the coconut milk, fill the can with water and add that, too. Add the tomatoes and dark chocolate, season with salt, then bring the liquid to a boil, lower the heat, and simmer for 30–40 minutes, until the tomatoes are breaking down.

Half-fill a large frying pan with sunflower oil and place it on medium–high heat. Pat the eggplants dry with a clean kitchen towel. Once the oil is hot (about 356°F/180°C on a cooking thermometer; or use the wooden-spoon test on page 244), fry the eggplants in batches for 3–4 minutes per batch, turning, until they are caramel all over. Remove each batch with a slotted spoon, transferring it to a wire rack over a baking sheet, to drain away any excess oil. Top up the oil, and bring it back to temperature before frying the next batch.

Once the tomatoes are ready in the saucepan, add your drained chickpeas, bring the liquid back to a simmer, cook for 10 minutes, then fold in your eggplants. Simmer for a final 10 minutes, so the eggplants have time to absorb the flavors, but without breaking apart. Then, serve.

Pepperpot is traditionally served on Christmas Day in Guyana—the only country in South America to have been a British colony, but with a culture that chimes with the Caribbean. The roots of this rich, hearty stew lead to Guyana's indigenous communities, who discovered that the liquid from the bitter cassava root, extracted in the process of making cassava flour, could be boiled with spices to result in a thick, dark sauce that could, in turn, be used as a natural preservative—cassareep. Without access to refrigeration, traditionally, the Guyanese stored their pans of pepperpot atop stoves, then reheated it daily (this is why an authentic version wouldn't contain onion, which would spoil the pepperpot over several days of reheating).

Some Guyanese variations of pepperpot call for a combination of beef, pork, and oxtail—I usually stick just to pork, but feel free to use a mixture to the same weight, if you prefer. Cassareep's flavor can vary wildly, but taste as you go and adjust your seasonings—including adding extra cinnamon, thyme, or cloves—to get the flavoring you prefer. I've also been known to add Green Seasoning (see page 36) to the marinade . . . although I can't say this is traditional, it adds a slight bitterness.

CURRIES, SOUPS, STEWS

My Pepperpot

For four

For the stew

1 lb 5 oz/600g skinless, boneless pork shoulder, cut into bite-sized pieces

3 tbsp sunflower oil, plus extra if needed

1 onion, diced

3 garlic cloves, finely chopped

2 green onions, thinly sliced

About 8 thyme sprigs

½ Scotch bonnet, seeded and finely chopped

Combine all the ingredients for the pepperpot marinade in a medium mixing bowl. Add the pork pieces and turn to coat them fully. Cover the bowl and place it in the fridge overnight. Take your pork out of the fridge a good 30–40 minutes before you intend to cook, to come up to room temperature.

Heat 1 tablespoon of the oil in a large Dutch oven on medium heat. In batches, add the pork pieces and brown them, turning, until they are evenly colored on all sides. Set each batch aside on a plate while you brown the next. Use a little water to deglaze the pan in between batches, pouring the deglazing water out and into a bowl each time. (When you're done, taste the water and as long as it's not bitter, keep it to use as stock; otherwise discard it.) Add an extra 1 tablespoon of oil, as needed, as you fry. Set aside the pork, deglaze the pan one last time, and wipe it clean.

1 tbsp black
  peppercorns
6 cloves
3-inch/7.5cm
  cinnamon stick
2 tsp demerara sugar
½ cup/120ml cassareep
2 cups/480ml chicken
  stock

For the marinade
½ tsp ground white
  pepper
3 garlic cloves, crushed
  to a paste
½ tsp dried thyme
1 tsp fine sea salt

Heat another 1 tablespoon of oil in your pot. Add the onion and sweat for 4–6 minutes, until almost softened. Add your garlic, green onions, thyme sprigs, and Scotch bonnet and fry for 1–2 minutes, then add your whole black peppercorns, cloves, and cinnamon stick. Fry for 1–2 minutes, then return the pork to the pot and add the sugar and cassareep. Mix everything thoroughly and then pour in the chicken stock.

Bring the liquid to a boil, then turn down the heat to a rolling simmer. Place the lid on the pot and cook for 1–1½ hours, until the meat is almost tender. Check the stew from time to time; if your sauce is looking a little thin, remove the lid after 1 hour and let it cook uncovered to reduce. If it's thickening quickly, add a little water to loosen. Serve the pepperpot hot with Buss Up Shut Roti (see page 175) and Fried Plantain (page 58) on the side.

This is a very good chicken curry; a curry that reminds me of Sundays, of comfort, of ease. My family was filled with much better meat-eaters than me—I ate only chicken, which meant on some Sundays we had roasted chicken or a mild chicken curry. Dad would listen to records while reading a paper, Richie would be upstairs playing video games, and Mum would be inspecting Dad's cooking. We had a cubby hole between the kitchen and living room that looked on to the dining table. I would be sitting on the sofa and see Dad going in to check on his dinner, making sure Mum wasn't interfering too much. I would catch them dancing, seeing Mum giggle at Dad's silliness. That's what this curry is for me—food at its simplest and most satisfying, Sundays captured in time.

CURRIES, SOUPS, STEWS

Mitchell Curry Chicken

For six (generously)

2 lb 2 oz/1kg skin-on, bone-in chicken, cut into 1¼–1½-inch/ 3–4cm pieces
1 tbsp sunflower oil
1 tbsp all-purpose flour
2 cups/480ml chicken stock
4 carrots, peeled and cut into ¾-inch/ 2cm slices
6 potatoes, cut into ¾-inch/2cm chunks

For the marinade
2 tsp fine sea salt
2 tbsp Jamaican Curry Powder (page 24)
16 black peppercorns
4 pimento berries
4 small–medium onions, finely diced
8 garlic cloves, finely chopped
¾ oz/20g ginger root, finely chopped
½ Scotch bonnet, seeded and diced
4 tbsp/60ml sunflower oil

Place your chicken pieces in a mixing bowl. Add all the ingredients for the marinade (leave out the Scotch bonnet if you like it mild) and mix well to make sure the meat is coated. Cover the bowl and place the chicken in the fridge overnight. Remove it 30–40 minutes before you intend to cook, to come up to room temperature.

To make the stew, heat a large Dutch oven or lidded frying pan on medium heat. In batches, add the chicken, doing your best to avoid adding the other ingredients in the bowl, and cook the meat for a couple of minutes, turning to seal in the spices and until it has taken on some color. Remove each batch to a plate while you brown the remainder. (Don't worry if some of your onion mixture gets into the pan—just remove it with the chicken as you go.)

Add the 1 tablespoon of sunflower oil to your pan. When it's hot, add the onion mixture from the marinating bowl and sweat it for about 5 minutes, stirring, until soft. Tip in the flour and cook for 2 minutes, stirring to cook it out. Gradually pour in your stock, stirring to incorporate the flour and remove any lumps. Nestle your chicken back into the pan and add your carrots and potatoes. Pour in enough water to just cover the chicken. Put the lid on and bring the liquid to a boil. Then, lower the heat and simmer, covered, for 30 minutes. Check the consistency. If the stew needs to thicken, cook for 10 minutes with the lid off; if not, leave the lid on for the remainder of the cooking time, until the chicken is cooked through and you can easily pierce your vegetables with a knife. Serve with plain rice.

163

Oxtail needs time. A long, slow cook will yield melt-in-the-mouth, falling-off-the-bone meat, which is one of the reasons it ended up in the roster of dishes coveted by Jamaicans, and more widely Caribbeans. Historically, meat would have been scarce on the islands, and oxtail wasn't favored by the upper classes. This meant it was readily available for enslaved Africans—cuts like oxtail would have been a lifeline for many of my ancestors. I wasn't one for meat when I was young, but freedom of choice is never lost on me. Watching my daughter eating meat as enthusiastically as my mum once did gives me a sense of their symmetry. I don't get to see that symmetry in motion, in real time, but I do get to imagine it. In my daughter, I feel I see so much of my mum, from a time I didn't know her.

Making this stew feels like a homage to those who have cooked it before me, and the passing down of intuitive skills, resilience, and power from one generation to the next. This dish highlights once again how from scarcity can come greatness.

CURRIES, SOUPS, STEWS

Low, Slow Oxtail Stew

For six

For the stew
2 lb 2 oz/1kg oxtail, trimmed and cut into 1½-inch/4cm chunks (ask your butcher to do this)
All-purpose flour, for coating the meat
2–3 tbsp sunflower oil
1 quart/1 liter chicken or beef stock
1 tbsp Worcestershire sauce
1 tbsp tomato paste
1 tbsp light brown sugar
2 carrots, peeled, and cut into ½-inch/1cm half moons
1 x 15-oz/425g can of butter beans (lima beans), drained
Fine sea salt

Place your oxtail pieces in a medium mixing bowl. Add all the ingredients for the marinade and mix well to make sure all the meat is coated. Cover the bowl and place the meat to marinate in the fridge overnight.

Remove the oxtail from the fridge 30–40 minutes before you intend to cook, to come up to room temperature. Extract the oxtail pieces, leaving the marinade in the bowl for later. Toss the pieces in a little flour to coat.

Heat 1 tablespoon of the oil in a medium pot on medium–high heat. When it's hot, add the meat in batches, doing your best to avoid adding the other ingredients in the bowl and turning to brown it on all sides, until it's got some nice color—you want a deep caramel. This will take about 10 minutes. Set aside each batch while you brown the remainder, adding more oil as you need. Feel free to deglaze the pot between batches if some of the seasonings stick on the bottom. Pour in a little water, and use a wooden spoon to scrape up all the caught flavor, then pour the contents back into the rest of the stock ready to use later. It all adds flavor to the dish. Otherwise, if you're not worried, no need to deglaze.

For the marinade

1½ tsp fine salt

4 green onions, finely diced

1 oz/30g ginger root, finely chopped

3–4 garlic cloves, minced

1 tbsp thyme leaves

2 onions, finely chopped

½ Scotch bonnet, seeded and minced

1 tbsp pimento berries

1 tbsp black peppercorns

2 tsp Top Spice Mix (page 23)

Once you've finished browning the meat, set it all aside and add another 1 tablespoon of the oil to the pot. When it's hot, add the onion mixture from the marinating bowl and sweat it for about 5 minutes, stirring, until soft. Then, add your Worcestershire sauce and tomato paste. Cook for 1 minute more, then tuck the oxtail back into the pot. Gradually pour in your stock and the reserved deglazing liquid (if you have it) to just cover the meat (you may not need all the stock—keep any extra for later, in case you need it) and add the sugar. Bring the liquid to a boil, add a pinch of salt to season, then lower the heat to a low simmer, put the lid on the pot and cook the stew low and slow for 2–3 hours, until the meat is almost tender. Lift the lid and stir the stew occasionally to make sure the meat isn't sticking—you can add a little more stock (or water) if it is.

After 2 hours, or when your meat is softening, add the carrots and drained butter beans and leave the lid off. Cook for 30 minutes, until the carrots are soft but still have some bite. If your sauce is too thick, thin it out with a little more stock or water before serving. Serve with Home Rice & Peas (see page 117) or steamed white rice.

We resist.

When our ancestors were taken by force to the Caribbean, they held on to what they could of the cultural practices from their old lives, which is how—as Candice Goucher wrote in her book *Congotay! Congotay!*—Caribbean food, with the "distinct cultures, peoples, and languages of four continents," became the first real global cuisine. This is the most important form of preservation practiced by our forebears—it is self-preservation. But when we think of preservation at its most basic, we think of it as a set of techniques to make food last for longer. Pickling, to prevent vegetables and fruit from spoiling; salting and brining, to arrest the decay of meat and fish; spicing, to slow spoiling and add flavor. Many of these processes allowed for cheap sustenance during the transatlantic slave trade, then the techniques weaved in to become tradition. Now, they are ubiquitous with the cuisine.

The diversity within Caribbean cuisine stems from the diversity of our ancestors, and it is often unappreciated or misunderstood. Much of what most people in the English-speaking world think of as Caribbean food comes from the English-speaking Caribbean, notably Jamaica, whose dominance comes from it being by far the largest of the former British colonies. The Caribbean region is vast—it's more than 1,500 miles from Cuba to Trinidad—and the idea that there wouldn't be variations in the cuisine makes no sense at all, even more so given the different European colonial powers and the length of the West African coastline from which millions of men, women, and children were trafficked. The cohesion that exists throughout the islands, and through their food, comes from shared experience—and this is why I think of the people of those islands as family.

During the era of plantation slavery, the market was one of the few places where the enslaved population could share ideas and swap news. The market was not only a place of trade, but also a place to nurture acts of resistance. Markets in the Caribbean, and diaspora communities throughout the world, are like their West African equivalents. They're busy, loud, and bustling, and exchanges take place between shoppers, not solely with traders. When I was a kid, we would often bump into friends and occasionally even family when out shopping on the weekends, at times dawdling for what felt like excessive amounts of time while Mum chatted away to someone or other. But nowadays many of these markets, which are essential social spaces in the Caribbean and places of sanctuary and opportunity for displaced people in the urban West, are threatened by gentrification and big business. Their continued existence reflects the commitment and in some cases resistance of the African and Caribbean women, right at the heart of their communities, who depend so heavily upon them.

I think of Caribbean food as bountiful, and this is surely partly down to the region's culture of generous hospitality. Colonization caused disruption in agricultural practices that were based around a connection and collaboration with the earth, where communities rarely went without— and the disruption continues to this day, even if it's not obvious to outsiders. In Grenada, I was surprised, shocked even, by how much food was imported—partly because of the expense to those who live on the island, but mainly (and naïvely) because I assumed that its fertile soil and warm climate would cultivate a varied abundance of produce. In fact, plenty of wonderful produce is grown there, on small plots of land, but it tends to be distributed via networks of those who sell directly to one another. This system is rooted in resistance, and preserves a tradition of self-reliance in the face of British policy, dating back to the time of slavery, to rely on imports—a policy that to this day still looms over the English-speaking Caribbean. The empire's role was to produce raw materials to be shipped back to the mother country to feed the factories there. The undermining of economic growth in the Caribbean is perhaps why these networks today remain hidden or underground—a legacy of a time when it was necessary to safeguard these behaviors.

Slavery was a period of enforced hunger, and it was through African agricultural know-how that the enslaved were sustained. African diets provided foundations that are still felt in the hard foods or ground provisions of the Caribbean today. For those unfamiliar with these terms—they are the starchy root vegetables, fruits, and dumplings that are boiled in salted water and served as side dishes or included in soups. Both rice and yam, which feature heavily in Caribbean diets today, would have formed the basis of many meals back in Africa. The Caribbean sweet potato was likely introduced by the Taínos, long before the arrival of the first slave ship. Plantain and banana made their way to the Caribbean via the slave trade, having previously been introduced to Africa through trade with Asia during the Trans-Saharan boom. Indigenous populations from Mexico brought corn. The Portuguese introduced cassava to Africa, following their colonization of Brazil, and subsequently transported it to the Caribbean through the transatlantic slave trade. Breadfruit originally came from Polynesia, imported by British plantation owners as a source of starchy sustenance for the enslaved population.

Although these staples weren't all heritage foods—in that they hadn't all originated in Africa—the cross-pollination of culture and history has made them integral to the way we think about Caribbean food today. The fact that they were easy to grow in relatively small areas, and nutritionally dense, made them an indispensable part of our ancestors' diets. Given that food is an unspoken expression of who we are to ourselves and to others, it's unsurprising that ground provisions to this day remain core to our culinary identity.

Dumplings, Buns, Breads.

Caribbean baking is sweet. One reason for that is
that many of the cuisines' breads include sugar, another
is the liberal use of spices. Walking past a Caribbean
bakery hits the senses in a way that is different to
a meander past any other—the wafting of earthy
spices catches you, and almost inevitably draws you in.
At Christmas and Easter, you'll see crowds of eager
devotees queuing up outside, to be sure of securing
the precious goods. We would always work a visit to the
bakery into the holiday planning—often my nan would
end up going for the entire extended family.

When it comes to Caribbean baked goods,
my devotion is complete. I eat bread so that I can
eat butter, and vice versa—it's a win-win situation.
Cooking (and eating) has always been my life, but baking
is my therapy. And while the recipes in this chapter are
perfect for mopping up curries, dipping in soups, or
stuffing with ackee and saltfish, they're also delicious
straight from the oven. The shapeshifting ability of dough
never ceases to amaze me—so much so that maybe
one day I'll dedicate an entire book to it.

Okay: this bread makes me weak at the knees. It's a love affair. As soon as I smell it baking, I'm in the back of Mum's red Ford Fiesta being told not to touch the warm, fresh loaf. Suddenly, I've ripped into it and have zero regrets.

This is not a bread that lingers. If, like me, you can't resist it warm from the oven, at least you'll have happy bread-based memories. It's the best bread for everything, but my top choice is a fried-egg-and-plantain sandwich, made with two generously thick slices, which my dad affectionately calls "doorstops." Or, a close second: one slice, with or without butter, topped with slices of avocado pear (but definitely slices—to mash the avocado would be a crime on this soft, doughy bed).

DUMPLINGS, BUNS, BREADS

Hard Dough Bread

Makes one loaf

3⅔ cups/450g all-
purpose flour, plus
extra for dusting
½ x ¼-oz/7g packet
of fast-acting
dried yeast
1½ tbsp light brown
sugar
1 tsp fine sea salt
2 tbsp unsalted butter
About 1 cup/240ml
tepid water
Sunflower oil,
for greasing

Combine all the dry ingredients in a medium mixing bowl. Add the butter and use a knife to cut it into the mixture, until it is in lots of small pieces. Mix everything together with your fingers, until you have a breadcrumb consistency. Then, little by little, incorporate the water, bringing the dough together into a ball that you can turn out to knead. You may not need all the water, but it's best to have it there in case you do.

Turn out the dough onto a lightly floured work surface and knead it for 15–20 minutes, until you have a smooth ball— you should be able to lightly press your finger into it and have it spring back. Grease the dough with sunflower oil, then place it in a clean bowl and cover the bowl with the lid of a pan. Let the dough rise somewhere warm for 40 minutes, until doubled in size.

Turn out the risen dough and knead it again for 5 minutes to knock it back.

Grease an 8½ x 4½-inch/22 x 11 cm loaf pan with oil and shape your dough into a loaf before gently pressing it in to the edges of the pan. Let it rise, uncovered, in a warm place for another 40 minutes, until it's risen out of the loaf pan.

Meanwhile, preheat your oven to 350°F. When the dough has risen, bake it for about 20 minutes, until the top is golden and the bottom of the loaf sounds hollow when tapped. Turn out the loaf and place it, right way up, on a wire rack to cool (or, rip off hunks of the bread and eat it warm).

Roti found its way to the Caribbean via indentured Indian laborers, a large Indian diaspora, with the biggest communities in Trinidad and Tobago and Guyana, who introduced foods like curries, roti, and chutneys to the region. The name "buss up shut" comes from the way the roti is beaten with wooden spatulas, spoons, and hands after cooking, breaking up the layers until it looks like a "bust-up shirt." Making roti is my therapy—my hands work and my mind rests. For that, I'm very thankful to Joe, who, for a number of years, was my (business) partner-in-crime with Island Social Club—if it weren't for him, I doubt roti would have become so integral to my cooking.

DUMPLINGS, BUNS, BREADS

Buss Up Shut Roti

For six

3½ cups/450g bread flour, plus extra for dusting
½ tbsp baking powder
½ tbsp fine sea salt
½ tbsp light brown sugar
1¼ cups/300ml hand-hot water, oat milk, or whole milk
½ tbsp sunflower oil
About 7 tbsp/100ml sunflower oil and 7 tbsp/100g melted ghee (have a bit extra, just in case), combined

Place all the dry ingredients into a large mixing bowl and stir to combine. Make a well in the center and pour in the water or milk. Using your fingers, gradually incorporate the dry ingredients into the liquid to form a wet dough.

Turn out the dough onto a lightly floured work surface and knead it for about 10 minutes, to a soft, springy ball that you can press lightly and have it spring back. Grease the dough with oil, then place it in a clean bowl. Cover, and let the dough rest at room temperature for 30 minutes.

Divide the dough into six equal balls. One by one, hold each ball in the palm of one hand and gently pinch the outer edge of the ball with your opposite hand, bringing it into the center. Repeat all around the ball edge. Use a thumb to press into the center to seal all the pinches together. Once you have sealed all the balls, oil them and rest them in your mixing bowl, covered with a kitchen towel, for another 30 minutes (you can place them on a baking sheet, if you prefer). Once they have rested, use your hands to gently flatten each ball and rotate it to form a fat disc.

A portion at a time, shape the roti. Using a rolling pin, roll each dough ball into a 6-inch/15cm disc, repeatedly rolling and turning 180 degrees for an even roll. Imagine the disc as a clock face. Slice the dough disc at 12 o'clock, making a vertical slit to the center. Brush the disc generously with your oil and ghee mixture, all the way to the edge, then pick up the right-hand cut edge and, in thirds, fold over the first half of the clock face, in a clockwise direction (2 o'clock to 4 o'clock to 6 o'clock). Then, roll the dough from the folded edge around the rest of the imaginary clock face (clockwise to 12), so that you finish with a tight, layered cone. Holding the cone in one hand, point downward, use your opposite thumb to push all the layers into the center to seal the end of the cone. Return the cone to the work surface, sealed end downward, and press in the pointed end to seal there, too. Repeat for each ball of dough.

Transfer the roti to the fridge and rest them for at least 4 hours, but ideally overnight, so you preserve those lovely layers. Alternatively, place the cones in an airtight container (side by side, but never stacked on top of one another, which would deform their shape) and freeze them for up to 3 months. (Alternatively, you can freeze them once they are rolled out, before cooking, and cook them from frozen.) Keep the remaining oil and ghee mixture for when you come to cook—you'll need to warm it a little to loosen it again for brushing.

When you're ready to cook, gently flatten the dough balls into a round and roll them out using the same motion of one direction at a time, repeatedly rotating 180 degrees to create a circular, flat roti, about 6 inches/15cm in diameter and ⅛–¼ inch/4–5mm thick (don't worry if it's not perfect— my roti rarely are). You don't want to roll too hard or too thin as you will then lose all the lovely layers.

Warm a tawa or frying pan on medium heat. When hot, brush the pan with your oil and ghee mixture and place your first roti on or in the pan. Oil the roti a little before flipping it over, you'll want to make sure it is nicely colored—no more than 30 seconds to 1 minute each side should be perfect. Then, beat each roti all over with your spatula until it starts to break up a little, before setting aside to keep warm while you repeat with the remaining dough. Once all the roti are cooked, serve them straightaway.

Boiled dumplings get the name spinners from the term "spinners and sinkers," which refers to the way you prepare the dough, and how the dumplings sink during cooking (Caribbean dumplings are denser than many other types). The spinning is, in essence, rubbing your hands back and forth, like you're plotting something, before releasing the dumplings into the liquid to cook. It's a rhythmic, ritualistic process.

We use all-purpose flour in our dumplings, but cornmeal features in the dumplings of others, so I've included both versions here. You can boil them in salted water to serve alongside ackee and saltfish (see page 54), stews, or fried fish; or boil them by dropping them into soups—as in the vegan Saturday Soup on page 142.

DUMPLINGS, BUNS, BREADS

Spinners

Makes twelve

For the plain version
¾ cup/100g all-
   purpose flour, plus
   extra for dusting
½ tsp fine sea salt
⅓ cup/80ml water
Sunflower oil,
   for greasing

**For the cornmeal
   version**
3 tbsp cornmeal
¾ cup/100g all-
   purpose flour, plus
   extra for dusting
½ tsp fine sea salt
⅓ cup/80ml water
Sunflower oil,
   for greasing

Sift the flour or flour and cornmeal into a mixing bowl and add the salt. Mix the dry ingredients together, make a well and, little by little, add the water (you may not need it all). Using your fingers, gradually incorporate the dry ingredients into the well to form a soft dough.

Turn out the dough onto a lightly floured work surface and knead it for about 5 minutes, to a soft, springy ball that you can press lightly and have it spring back. Grease the dough with oil, then place it in a clean bowl. Cover, and let the dough rest at room temperature for 10 minutes.

Divide the rested dough into twelve equal pieces, and shape each one into a ball. Take each ball and rub it back and forth between your palms to make a little spinner— a thin sausage shape. It should be about ½ inch/1cm thick, but you can make them whatever size you prefer, you'll just need to adjust the cooking time to suit. Once you have rolled all the spinners, bring a pot of salted water to a boil. Pop the spinners into the pot and cover with a lid. Cook for 10–15 minutes, or until the spinners start to float.

Alternative: If you like, you can make dumpling discs rather than spinners. Flatten the balls into discs, cook them in salted water as above, and enjoy like that. If you have any left over, carefully cut them in half horizontally, then fry them in a little oil until they turn brown at the edges (2–3 minutes each side). I love serving these with the Sticky BBQ Ribs (see page 98). We used to have them as a kid and they get the crispiest edges and, with that gravy, they're outrageous!

Hands down, my nan makes the best fried dumplings. I asked her to teach me once. Her hands moved gracefully, speedily, wrist flicking, spinning little balls of dough into perfect rounds that she delicately layered around the edge of a Dutch oven. I'm still trying to get that technique down—I suspect it will take a few years yet. Attempting to lock down measurements for some of these recipes has been hard. Like a lot of diasporic cultures, you watch your nan/mum/dad/auntie and, if you ask for specifics, they simply say, "a likkle this, a likkle that," and even my beady eye rarely catches what "likkle" might be. To try to make sense of what is so instinctual, I've given you two versions. I like lighter dumplings; the hubs likes them denser. Double up the recipe to make more.

DUMPLINGS, BUNS, BREADS

Nan's Fried Dumplings

Makes four

For dense dumplings

2 cups/250g all-
   purpose flour
1 tbsp baking powder
¾ tsp fine sea salt
½ tsp light brown sugar
¾ cup plus 2 tbsp/
   200ml water
¾ cup plus 2 tbsp/
   200ml sunflower oil,
   for frying

For airy dumplings

2 cups/250g all-
   purpose flour
½ tsp baking powder
½ tsp fine sea salt
½ tsp light brown sugar
¾ cup plus 2 tbsp/
   200ml sunflower oil,
   for frying, plus 1 tsp
   for the mixture
¾ cup plus 2 tbsp/
   200ml water

For either version, sift all the dry ingredients into a medium mixing bowl. Make a well in the center and, for the airy dumplings, add the 1 teaspoon of oil. Have the water at the ready—you may not use it all. Little by little, pour water into the middle of the well, using your fingers to incorporate it into the dry ingredients until you can bring the mixture together in a ball. Turn the dough out of the bowl and knead it for not more than 3–4 minutes, until the dough springs back quickly when you press it with a finger. Return the dough to the bowl, cover with a kitchen towel, and let it rest at room temperature for 20 minutes.

Divide the rested dough into four equal pieces, form each piece into a ball, then flatten it in the palm of your hands. One by one, gently pinch all around the outer edge of each ball, bringing the pinch into the center each time. I cup the ball in my left hand and pinch and fold in with my right. Then, I pinch the center as if making a pleat and push the pleat into the ball with my thumb, sealing the dough back together. Rest the dough balls, uncovered, for 5 minutes.

Heat the sunflower oil in a Dutch oven or frying pan on medium heat (make sure it doesn't come more than halfway up the side). The oil is hot enough when a little of the dumpling dough bubbles up when you drop it in. Turn the heat down to medium–low so that the dumplings cook from the inside out and don't burn, and add the dumplings, turning them as they start to puff. Cook for 4–5 minutes, until they are a medium golden color. Remove them with a slotted spoon and drain them on a plate or baking sheet lined with parchment paper.

I first made these buns to serve with "Shark" Hake Bites (see page 70) at a supper club for around seventy people. I was doing most of the prep with just my dad and I didn't sleep for two days. I wanted to make every bun by hand but, because I was so tired, I had burned all my yeast in my first attempts. I almost gave up and bought pre-made buns, but I couldn't. So, at 4am on the day of the event, I found an open supermarket and bought more yeast and tried again. I made the buns, and the buns banged. With the hake bites, they're so good. Now, they remind me of overcoming adversity to deliver an imperfect perfect night: the food was late (the pots, pans, plates, and glasses disappeared; the ovens stopped working), but the evening was balmy, and the soundtrack of bashment and soca music added to the perfect imperfection.

DUMPLINGS, BUNS, BREADS

Coco Bread Buns

Makes six

3¼ cups/400g white
   bread flour, sifted,
   plus extra for dusting
1½ tsp fine sea salt
¾ cup plus 3 tbsp/
   225ml full-fat
   coconut milk mixed
   with 2 tbsp water
1½ tbsp light brown
   sugar
1 x ¼-oz/7g packet
   of fast-acting
   dried yeast
1 egg, lightly beaten
Sunflower oil,
   for greasing
3 tbsp unsalted butter,
   melted

Sift the flour and salt into a medium mixing bowl. Set aside.

In a small saucepan on low heat, very gently heat your coconut milk and water mixture until it's just lukewarm (about 68°F/20°C)—this won't take more than a few seconds, we're just taking the chill off to activate the yeast. Pour the milk into a separate mixing bowl and add the sugar and yeast and whisk to dissolve. Whisk in the beaten egg.

Make a well in the center of your flour and salt mixture and pour in the wet ingredients. Using your fingers, gradually incorporate the dry ingredients into the well to form a soft dough. Tip out the dough onto a lightly floured surface and knead it to a smooth ball—roughly 10 minutes should do it. Oil your dough, place it in a clean mixing bowl, and cover it with a damp kitchen towel. Let the dough rise in a warm place for 1 hour, or until doubled in size.

Tip out the risen dough onto a lightly floured surface and knead it for 5 minutes to knock it back. Divide the dough into six equal pieces, then form each piece into a ball. One by one, use a rolling pin to roll each ball into a 6-inch/15cm disc. Brush each disc with melted butter and then fold it in half to form a semicircle. Brush the top with butter and let the semicircles rest, uncovered, at room temperature for 30 minutes. Meanwhile, preheat your oven to 400°F.

Transfer the buns, spaced well apart, to a baking sheet lined with parchment paper (you may need two sheets), and lower the oven to 350°F. Bake the buns for 20–30 minutes, until puffed and golden.

Cornbread comes in many guises, conjuring thoughts of the deep South or Latin American food, fried chicken and collard greens, tamales and tortillas, but it is also represented in both African and Caribbean cultures. When enslaved Africans arrived in the Caribbean, corn replaced yam and other provisions, and became often used to make baked puddings and porridge.

Cornbread has evolved alongside industrialization—what once would have been made solely from corn and without any added sugar now features both wheat flour and sweeteners, turning the more pone-like bread, once white, to cakeish yellow. And, today, it has many versions. This one is mostly used as a savory food, although it is sweeter and more bread-like than its earliest Caribbean forebears. I have been known to eat it with chile jam and ice cream—don't judge . . . a wonderful critic did once (no hard feelings, Jimi Famurewa)—but, more usually, it features on rotation for our weekend breakfasts, alongside plantain and eggs or with pickles and jerk wings, nodding to that Southern charm, but rich with Caribbean sentimentality.

DUMPLINGS, BUNS, BREADS

Cornbread

For eight

1 cup/125 all-purpose flour
⅔ cup/100g cornmeal
Packed ⅔ cup/140g light brown sugar
1½ tsp fine sea salt
1 tbsp baking powder
1 cup/240ml whole milk, or full-fat coconut milk if you want it sweeter
5 tbsp/70ml light sunflower oil, plus extra (or butter) for cooking in a skillet
2 eggs, well beaten

Preheat the oven to 400°F. If you're using a 10-inch/25cm skillet, put that in the oven to heat up, too. If you're using a cake pan (I prefer a 10-inch/25cm square one), line the bottom and sides with parchment paper.

Combine all the dry ingredients in a mixing bowl, then mix in the milk and sunflower oil. Finally, fold the eggs into the mixture until everything is well combined and smooth.

If you're using a skillet, remove it from the oven (don't forget to use oven mitts, it'll be hot), then drop a knob of butter or about ½ tablespoon of oil into the pan and spread it evenly around the pan before pouring the mixture in. If you're using a lined cake pan, simply pour in the mixture.

Bake the cornmeal in the oven for 20–25 minutes, or until a skewer inserted into the center comes out clean. Serve warm in wedges for breakfast, with a fried egg, Fried Plantain (see page 58), and Hot Pepper Sauce (page 40), or I love to have it with the Honey Jerk Wings on page 73.

My first attempts at making a vegan pumpkin bread turned out like cake. Then, I stumbled across a Dan Lepard recipe . . . but even that I managed to butcher. Some expletives were uttered, some tinkering was done, and I finally made a near-perfect loaf. Then, a friend asked for the recipe and I promised to send it. To this day, I have no idea where my original notes are—I have a bad habit of writing on envelopes—but after more months of tinkering, more expletives, and an internet deep-dive, I found the original recipe and began the tinkering process all over again. The result is this irresistible bread which, given its heft, is guaranteed to disappear surprisingly soon.

DUMPLINGS, BUNS, BREADS

Squash & Thyme Bread

For one large loaf

9 oz/250g peeled and seeded pumpkin or squash, cut into chunks
2 tbsp thyme leaves, plus 5 sprigs for the pumpkin/squash
¾ cup/180ml tepid water
1 x ¼-oz/7g packet of fast-acting dried yeast
6 tbsp/100g Greek soy (or dairy) yogurt
4¾ cups/600g white bread flour, sifted, plus extra for dusting
2 tsp fine sea salt
1 tbsp sunflower oil

Bring a medium saucepan of salted water to a boil. Add the pumpkin or squash chunks and whole thyme sprigs and boil for 10–15 minutes, until the chunks are soft. Drain, discarding the thyme sprigs, and tip the veg into a mixing bowl. Using a potato masher, mash the pumpkin or squash and then transfer it to a baking sheet to cool for 10 minutes before placing it in the fridge to chill for 10 minutes, until it is just warm to the touch—if you have a cooking thermometer, you want it to be around 68°F/20°C to activate the yeast.

Remove the bowl from the fridge and whisk in the tepid water before whisking in your yeast until dissolved. Mix in the yogurt, then add the flour, salt, thyme leaves, and oil, mixing to form a soft dough.

Tip out the dough onto a lightly floured work surface and knead it until it is smooth and quite firm (the salt will draw moisture from the dough, making it softer as it rises). Return the dough to the bowl, cover with a kitchen towel or plastic wrap, and let it rise in a warm place for 1 hour, until risen by half.

Tip out the risen dough onto your work surface and shape it into a round or stubby oval. Transfer it to a baking sheet lined with parchment paper and score it with a blunt knife or dough scraper, then cover it with a kitchen towel or oiled plastic wrap. Put it back in to your warm spot for 1 hour, until risen again.

Preheat your oven to 425°F. Bake the loaf for about 30 minutes, until it's deep golden on top and the bottom sounds hollow when tapped.

We flourish.

My journey into cooking began in earnest on the eve of my thirtieth birthday, borne out of a desire to understand myself and my history. It's a journey I will always be on, and I wouldn't have it any other way. Its pathways have connected me with a community of fellow diasporans, who are themselves crafting their own connections to their roots. It feels as though I'm part of a loose movement, one that is centered on re-rooting back in the Caribbean or Africa, rather than assimilating outside of it. Personally, I feel such peace when I'm back "home." I've loved growing up and living in London, a city of many shades; but there have been big negatives, too. When I'm in the Caribbean, I exist as a person, without the need for Black to frame my identity.

But there remain deep wounds in the Caribbean, and perhaps the deepest and darkest of them derive from sugar. This luxury product stole the lives of millions through its agonizing, back-breaking, dangerous cultivation, and continues to take its toll as a cause of ill health, including diabetes and other life-threatening conditions. And yet—I would not have found my way to cooking without sugar, with so much of what I most enjoy making including it, and so many of the most joyous aspects of Caribbean culture coming from it, too. Bakes, cakes, pickles, punch. We have a complicated relationship with sugar. It's a constant reminder of a painful past, but it's also a product that we use to celebrate our joy and resilience—especially when we consume it as rum!

It's no coincidence, I think, that the more we chase after success in a world where it is measured in financial wealth, the less connected we feel to ourselves and each other. We need to find new ways to connect, new ways to establish our sense of community. The longer the passing of time since our move from the Caribbean—in our displaced communities, the more diluted our culture becomes, and that dilution is really a loss of community. I think this is why we are now seeing a shift toward people returning, or at least spending more time back *home*. There's a word in Ghanaian, *sankofa* ("to retrieve"), that appears in a proverb to remind us of the virtue in returning to collect what we've forgotten. The notion of *sankofa* is often depicted as a bird, with its feet planted firmly forward, its head facing backward, and an egg in its beak. The image represents how important it is to look back at your past, and to carry the lessons learned (symbolized by the egg, a powerhouse of knowledge and possibility) with you into the future. An illustration of the bird proudly decorates the cover of this book.

There are many ways to contribute positively as a human being, and there are many ways of doing so as a Caribbean person, and all deserve to be celebrated. But imagine if no hierarchies existed, or we found ways to redefine our culture that transcended the legacies of empire and colonialism? Where we could work without hindrance on rectifying the injustices of the past, moving culture and conversations forward. Happily, these days I see more of us telling our own stories and being heard for the first time by those outside our community. For so long, we were denied a platform to share these stories, or told that we could share them only when someone else stepped down from the platform. There's space for us all—we don't need to be set against one another.

I have also loved witnessing how so many of my contemporaries are capturing and sharing traditions that have been at risk of being lost. So much of this comes from shifting perceptions of what is deemed worthy of being maintained, and otherwise might be lost through assimilation. Certainly, being part of a diaspora community means I carry influences from multiple worlds—a free-flowing dilution that feels inevitable, and that I've come to accept.

I feel keenly that those of my parents' and grandparents' generations kept boxed up so much of their precious, fundamental identity, protecting it fiercely and sharing it only in private, and even then, rarely. It feels poignant to me that those of us from immigrant ancestors, who are redefining what it means to be Caribbean, are doing so unapologetically. This wasn't something that felt safe to the older generation and, if I am honest, it's not always felt safe to me either. I remember how animated Mum was after watching Steve McQueen's *Small Axe*—she spoke about it for days. The *Lovers Rock* episode, especially, reminded her of the parties that were often the only spaces my parents could be fully free to express themselves and their culture. As a kid, I'd see snippets of that self-expression—usually at a wedding or celebration in a community hall in South London. Music would be pumping from vast speakers, and I would catch my parents lost in one another, as if no one else were around. I was young, and therefore disgusted by my parents' public display of affection! I would make a disapproving face and move on. I see now how utterly special those moments were.

We should never feel it necessary to deny our culture anywhere. Why should it be that when others access culture through appropriation, it's deemed cool, but when culture is expressed organically, it's considered problematic? It's fitting, perhaps, given the lack of investment in industry and infrastructures that left the former British sugar islands in a state of collapse, that the strongest export of the Caribbean these days should be its culture. Our food, our music, our sportsmanship, our fashion—our continued ingenuity, our ability to fan a creative spark until it ignites. It's why we are so fiercely protective of our culture; it is so much of who we are. We are prideful because our culture could not be stripped away from us.

Sweets, Desserts, Cakes.

Caribbean desserts are traditionally cake- or
sweet-based, with shaved ice and syrup also
a top draw. For many of the recipes in this chapter,
I've used ingredients and flavor combinations that satisfy
a deep nostalgia in me: stout punch, ginger
with lime, coconut and pineapple. I've used these
to create ice cream, cheesecake, and panna cotta,
but with a Caribbean inflection.

I always used to joke that I had two bellies—one for
savory and one for sweet. I think I might even have
convinced myself of it. The capacity I once had for
desserts! I now recall this as the hunger of youth.
My tastes have matured with age, and these days
I prefer my desserts to be subtly sweet, rather than
super-sweet—a journey that is reflected in many of these
recipes. I also wanted to honor some dishes that mean a
lot to me for sentimental reasons: Toto Coconut Loaf (see
page 196), the smell of which takes me back
to being seven years old; and the Custard Apple Sorbet
(see page 213) that Mum would have lost her mind over,
given how much she adored the fruits from back home.

Lemon drizzle, delicious; ginger drizzle, sensational. My personal opinion—and also a fact. Why? Because for the ginger lovers among us, the spice adds both pepperiness and subtle warmth. Use plenty of it—the result is balanced, moist, and effortlessly irresistible. I took my test loaf to the in-laws and it was gone by the end of the afternoon. I think that's a fairly good assessment of how good it is. You can add icing, for the sake of looks, or leave the loaf naked. Either way, sit down and have a moment with a cake that's not likely to last long after baking.

SWEETS, DESSERTS, CAKES

Ginger Drizzle

For eight

1 cup/225g unsalted
    butter, softened
1 cup plus 2 tbsp/225g
    granulated sugar
3 eggs, well beaten
1¾ cups plus 1 tbsp/
    225g all-purpose flour
2¾ tsp baking powder
½ tsp salt
2½ tsp ground ginger
Zest of 1 lime
⅓ oz/10g ginger root,
    peeled and grated
½ cup/120ml Ginger
    Syrup (page 223)

**For the drizzle and
    topping (optional)**
⅔ cup/85g golden
    powdered sugar
2–3 tsp water or ginger
    kombucha
Pinch of ground ginger
    (optional)
A few pieces of
    crystallized ginger
    (optional), chopped

Preheat the oven to 350°F. Line a 9 x 5-inch/23 x 12cm loaf pan (bottom and ends) with parchment paper.

Put the butter and sugar in a mixing bowl and, using a wooden spoon, cream them together until they are light and fluffy (you can do this using an electric beater, if you prefer). Fold in the eggs, one third at a time, then sift in the flour, baking powder, salt, and ground ginger. Use your wooden spoon to fold the dry ingredients into the wet mixture using a figure-eight motion, which combines but helps to avoid over-mixing—the less mixing, the more airy your cake. Add the lime zest and grated ginger root, then mix again until evenly distributed. Spoon the mixture into the lined loaf pan and level the top with the back of a spoon.

Bake the loaf on the middle shelf for 45–50 minutes, until risen and golden and a skewer inserted into the center comes out clean. Remove the loaf from the oven and allow it to cool in the pan for 5 minutes. Then, while it's still warm, poke a few holes in the top of the cake with a skewer and pour the ginger syrup over the top, letting it soak in as the loaf cools fully in the pan.

While the loaf is cooling, make the drizzle (if using). Sift the powdered sugar into a bowl, add the ground ginger (if using), and, little by little, add the water or ginger kombucha until you have a smooth icing with a drizzle consistency (you want it to be loose enough to run down the side of the cake, but not so loose it doesn't cover it).

Remove the loaf from the pan and place it on a serving plate. Pour the drizzle over the top, covering the top of the loaf and letting it run down the sides. Scatter the pieces of crystallized ginger (if using) and serve in slices.

Few of my childhood memories are more warming than Rebecca and her coconut cake. Rebecca was my nanny. When I got home from school, she would often give me a corn-and-scrambled-egg sandwich, followed—if I was lucky—by a slice of my favorite cake. When I walked into the house, my nose would twitch to catch whether she'd been baking. If she had, there was no hiding my eagerness for what was to come. That cake was heavenly—gently spiced, full of coconut. Given the chance, I would have eaten the entire thing in one sitting. As Rebecca was Saint Lucian, I assumed that her cake was too, but my research into its origins lead me to a Jamaican cake called toto. I made it, hoping it would be everything I had remembered. After many, many years without a piece of Rebecca's cake, I closed my eyes and was seven years old again—an age when a warm slice of toto was as good as life could get.

If you can't find fresh coconut, you can use unsweetened dried shredded coconut. To make the cake vegan, use vegan butter and milk, omit the egg and add an extra tablespoon of vegan milk and one more teaspoon of baking powder.

SWEETS, DESSERTS, CAKES

Toto Coconut Loaf

For eight

6 tbsp/85g unsalted butter, cubed, at room temperature, plus extra for greasing
1 cup/85g freshly grated or unsweetened dried shredded coconut
½ cup plus 2 tbsp/ 125g granulated sugar
2 eggs
2 tsp vanilla extract
1½ cups/200g all-purpose flour
Pinch of salt
2 tsp baking powder
1 tsp grated nutmeg
½ tsp pumpkin pie spice
Pinch of allspice
1 tsp ground cinnamon
½ cup/120ml whole milk

Preheat the oven to 375°F. Line a 9 x 5-inch/23 x 12cm loaf pan (bottom and ends) with parchment paper and grease the parchment with butter.

If you're using dried coconut, tip it onto a plate and place it in a steamer. Steam it for 10 minutes, then remove the steamer from the heat and carefully remove the plate with the coconut on—it'll be very hot. Set aside to cool.

Put the butter and sugar in a mixing bowl and, using a wooden spoon, cream them together until they are light and fluffy (you can do this using an electric beater, if you prefer). Add the eggs, and beat them into the mixture, taking care to retain as much air as possible. Beat in the vanilla, then sift in the flour, salt, baking powder, and spices and fold until just combined (take care not to over-mix). Finally, stir in the milk and coconut until fully incorporated and you have a smooth cake batter. Pour the batter into the loaf pan and bake it in the middle of your oven for 1 hour, until risen and golden and a skewer inserted into the center comes out clean. Allow the loaf to cool slightly in the pan, then remove it and serve it warm in slices.

This banana bread is best when you use the blackest of fruit. We had a glut of about thirty wildly overripe bananas from the early days of parenthood that I froze and slowly worked my way through for the best part of a year. The quest for sustainability starts at home, and I never follow sell-by dates, preferring the mighty sniff test, or using the freezer to save me from myself. Neither too sweet, nor too banana-y, this recipe features a smattering of dark chocolate on top, which offers a very nice bitterness; as does the sea salt, if you opt to use it.

To make a vegan version, just use vegan butter and non-dairy milk and omit the egg, but use three teaspoons of baking powder instead of two, which ensures a good rise and creates a nice, crispy topping with a light and airy inside.

Best Banana Bread

(BECAUSE IT IS)

For eight

½ cup plus 1 tbsp/125g
  unsalted butter, plus
  extra for greasing
½ cup/100g dark
  muscovado sugar
2 tsp vanilla extract
3 ripe bananas (the
  riper the better)
¼ cup/60ml whole milk
1½ cups/190g all-
  purpose flour
4¼ tsp baking powder
½ tsp salt
1 egg, beaten
⅓ oz/10g 70% dark
  chocolate, roughly
  chopped
Pinch of flaky sea salt
  (optional)

Preheat the oven to 350°F. Grease a 9 x 5-inch/23 x 12cm loaf pan with butter and line it (bottom and ends) with parchment paper.

Melt the butter with the sugar and vanilla extract in a small saucepan on medium–low heat. Meanwhile, mash your bananas in a medium mixing bowl. Pour the melted butter and sugar into the bananas and whisk to combine. Add the milk and stir well.

Combine the flour, baking powder, and salt in a separate bowl and sift the mixture into your banana batter, mixing slowly, until fully combined. Gently fold in the egg until incorporated. Pour the batter into the prepared loaf pan, then sprinkle with the chopped chocolate (I like making patterns with mine) and the sea salt (if using).

Bake the banana loaf for 40 minutes to 1 hour, depending on your oven, until the loaf is risen and a skewer inserted into the center comes out clean. It's a wet cake mixture, so don't be tempted to remove the cake from the oven too soon—if the top is getting too dark, place foil over it and keep baking until the center leaves no residue on the skewer. Let the loaf cool in the pan for about five minutes, then take it out of the pan, and slice it—it's especially delicious while it's still warm.

Sweet potato pudding was traditionally made outside on top of a coal stove, with coals above the cooking pot as well as below, making a dessert that was "Hell a-top, hell a-bottom, and hallelujah in the middle." This version is baked in an oven. Use a Caribbean sweet potato, which has white flesh and red skin, and may be called boniato or batata. It's starchier than European varieties (which aren't a workable swap), so much sturdier to cook with. This is *very* good with the rum cream given in the recipe on page 210, or with the Stout Punch Ice Cream on page 209.

SWEETS, DESSERTS, CAKES

Sweet Potato Pudding

For eight to ten

1 lb 3 oz/550g
   Caribbean sweet
   potatoes (boniato),
   peeled and cut into
   ¾-inch/2cm chunks
¾ cup plus 2 tbsp/
   200ml coconut milk
2 tbsp unsweetened
   dried shredded
   coconut
1 tbsp vanilla extract
½ tbsp dark rum
1 cup/125g all-purpose
   flour
Packed ⅓ cup/75g
   dark brown sugar
1 tsp baking powder
Scant ½ cup/60g raisins
⅓ cup/40g fine
   cornmeal
½ tsp fine sea salt
½ tsp pumpkin pie spice
Pinch of allspice
1 tsp ground ginger
1 tsp grated nutmeg

Preheat the oven to 375°F. Grease, then line a 9-inch/23cm springform cake pan with parchment paper. Bring a large saucepan of salted water to a boil. Add the sweet potato chunks and boil them for about 10 minutes, until soft. Drain and set aside to cool (10–15 minutes).

Meanwhile, pour the coconut milk into a mixing bowl, and add the dried shredded coconut, vanilla, and rum. Mix together and allow the coconut to rehydrate. Tip the flour, sugar, baking powder, raisins, cornmeal, salt, and ground spices into another mixing bowl and whisk to coat the raisins.

Tip the cooled sweet potato into the bowl with the coconut mixture, then mash everything together until smooth. Fold in the flour mixture, stir to combine, then pour the batter into your cake pan and bake for 1 hour 20 minutes, or until a skewer inserted into the center comes out clean.

While the pudding is baking, put all the caramel ingredients in a small saucepan on medium heat. Gently whisk to melt the butter and sugar. Then, turn up the heat and let the mixture bubble until it's reduced by half, or you have a nice, thick, pouring caramel (15–20 minutes). Remove from the heat and let cool while the pudding finishes baking.

For the caramel

2½ cups/600ml coconut milk

Packed ½ cup/105 g dark brown sugar

¼ tsp fine sea salt

2 tsp vanilla extract

½ tsp pumpkin pie spice

Pinch of allspice

½ tsp ground cinnamon

¼ cup/55g unsalted butter

An hour into the baking time, pour the caramel over the top and return the pudding to the oven for 20 minutes to finish cooking. Remove the pudding from the oven and let it cool in the pan. Then, place a kitchen towel over the top of the pan and pop the pudding in the fridge for at least 4 hours (but up 4 days), until set. Release the pudding from the pan and carefully transfer it to a serving plate. Serve chilled or at room temperature, in slices.

Some of the boujee peeps among us might write off a piña colada, but I don't feel like I've been in the Caribbean unless I've sat on a beach drinking one. The cocktail was created by a Puerto Rican, in Puerto Rico—a fact I did not know until some time after I'd visited Cuba (where I thought it came from) in 2016, on a research trip centered specifically around this cocktail. Naturally this well-researched trip led to a Cuban-themed supper club, where I had to include a riff on my favorite tipple. Enter my Piña Panna Cotta. This is a dessert that's all about nostalgia, and pairing rum with delicious creamy things. Before you begin, make sure the brand of gelatin you're using states that one packet (2¼ tsp) would set 2 cups/480ml of liquid (feel free to use a vegetarian gelatin if you like).

SWEETS, DESSERTS, CAKES

Piña Panna Cotta

WITH CARAMELIZED PINEAPPLE

For six

Coconut oil,
   for greasing
1¼ cups/300ml
   half-and-half
1½ x ¼-oz/7g packets
   of powdered gelatin
   (3⅓ tsp total)
1 x 13.5-oz/400ml can
   of full-fat coconut milk
2 tbsp light brown sugar
Up to 3 tbsp dark rum
Up to 1 tsp vanilla
   extract

**For the caramelized
   pineapple**
¼ cup/55g unsalted
   butter
2 tbsp light brown sugar
¼ pineapple, cored
   and cut into
   ¼-inch/5mm chunks
Grated nutmeg, to taste,
   plus extra to serve

Grease six individual pudding molds with coconut oil if you want to turn out your panna cottas; otherwise, use six individual dessert dishes.

Pour ¼ cup/60ml of the half-and-half in a small bowl. Sprinkle the gelatin over the half-and-half and let it soak for about 5 minutes. While the gelatin is soaking, place the coconut milk, remaining 1 cup/240ml half-and-half, and sugar in a saucepan on medium–low heat, stirring to dissolve the sugar. Take the pan off the heat and stir the soaked gelatin mixture into the warm milk until dissolved. Strain the mixture through a sieve into a clean bowl. Stir in the rum and vanilla to taste. Pour the mixture equally into your molds or dishes. Chill for at least 4 hours, or until set.

For the caramelized pineapple, melt the butter in a frying pan on medium heat. Add the sugar, stir to combine, then cook on medium–high heat, until the sugar has dissolved. Add your pineapple and cook, stirring from time to time to make sure it doesn't stick, until any liquid has evaporated, the sauce has thickened, and the pineapple is nicely coated. Add the nutmeg to taste and let cool.

To turn out the molded panna cottas, dip each mold for no longer than 30 seconds in hot water and invert each on to a serving plate. Serve with the caramelized pineapple and sauce drizzled over the top and an extra grating of nutmeg.

During Island Social Club, I found it shocking how few people ordered dessert. As a result, we offered only a small selection—sometimes even only one dessert at a time. One summer evening, a UK hip-hop artist with Guyanese heritage came to eat with us. He ordered this cheesecake, and loved it so much that he later featured it on the popular *Off Menu* podcast. His listeners went wild for it—from the day the podcast was released and for many weeks after that, we had to keep the cheesecake on our menu, even bringing it back on after attempting something new.

As someone who enjoys a dessert and who often treats it as a palate cleanser (even sticky toffee pudding), I prefer to offer those that aren't too heavy, that are subtle with their sweetness and that leave the diner wanting more (rather than feeling regretfully full). This unbaked cheesecake is light, and the lime and ginger are made for each other—the acidity in the lime and the warmth of the ginger provide real freshness. If you don't believe me, ask Loyle Carner.

SWEETS, DESSERTS, CAKES

Chilled Cheesecake

WITH GINGER SYRUP & LIME

For four

4½ oz/130g graham crackers
¼ cup/50g unsalted butter
5¼ oz/150g full-fat cream cheese
1 lime, finely grated zest and juice, plus optional extra zest to decorate
2 tbsp Ginger Syrup (page 223)
7 tbsp/100ml heavy cream

Crush the graham crackers in a food processor, or pop them in a ziplock bag and bash them with a rolling pin (it's very satisfying!). You're aiming for a relatively fine crumb. Tip them into a medium mixing bowl.

Melt the butter in a small saucepan, on medium–low heat. Pour the melted butter into the bowl with the cracker crumbs and stir to evenly coat the crumbs. Spoon an equal amount of your buttery crumbs into four ramekins or bowls, giving them a little shake to flatten the bottom without pressing it down. You don't want it too densely packed. Set aside.

In a clean bowl, mix together the cream cheese, lime zest and juice, and ginger syrup. Set aside.

Whip the heavy cream to a medium–firm peak, then fold this into the cream-cheese mixture. Spoon the mixture equally into the ramekins or bowls on top of the crumb base and use the back of a spoon to tidy it up in a swirl. Refrigerate the cheesecakes for 2–4 hours (depending on your fridge temperature), until set (it won't set firm, just thicken up).

Remove the cheesecakes from the fridge about 10 minutes before you intend to serve and grate some extra lime zest over the top, to decorate, if you wish.

A wise person once told me, "If it's not 60 percent, it's not chocolate—it's candy." She worked at the chocolate museum in Grenada, so I feel she should know . . . You need to use a good-quality chocolate for this mousse, and I advise a velvety Caribbean one. I include both the pulp and the seeds from the passionfruit for texture, but if you don't fancy that, eat the seeds and use four passionfruits-worth of pulp. Have everything ready to go so you can work quickly without stress— you don't want your chocolate to get too cool, but neither do you want to use it as soon as you remove it from the heat. You might think the results are very rich, but they're not—they're very smooth.

SWEETS, DESSERTS, CAKES

Chocolate Mousse

WITH TANGY PASSIONFRUIT

For four

3½ oz/100g 60–70% dark chocolate, plus extra to decorate
2 tbsp granulated sugar
4 eggs, separated
2–4 passionfruit (depending on your love of passionfruit), pulp and seeds scooped out

Melt the chocolate in a bowl over a pot of barely simmering water, making sure the bowl isn't touching the water. Remove from the heat and set aside.

Place the sugar in a clean mixing bowl with the egg whites and whisk them until you have soft peaks—they should flop over easily once you stop whisking.

In a separate bowl, whisk the egg yolks to break them down, then fold in your melted chocolate. Whisk until the color is even and the mixture is looking nice and thick.

Add the passionfruit to the chocolate-and-egg mixture and stir it in. Fold in a spoonful of the egg white to loosen (this is a sacrificial spoonful, so you don't have to be too precious when mixing it in). Then, one third at a time, carefully fold in the reminder of your egg whites—be gentle so as not to lose all the air from the mixture (I like to use a metal spoon or spatula and go straight down the middle before folding around, then rotating the bowl to repeat).

Divide the mousse mixture equally among four ramekins or individual serving dishes and transfer them to the fridge to chill for at least 4 hours, or until set. Serve decorated with fine gratings of dark chocolate.

I'm ashamed to admit that I like Guinness only when it has something sweet thrown in. (What can I say? I have a sweet tooth.) I didn't think there could be anything better than a Guinness punch, but turning it into ice cream has really made my lactose intolerance scream in exquisite anguish. Mixing a boozy, malty drink with rich, creamy custard is what my dreams are made of. Homemade ice cream takes a bit of work, mostly in the form of patience, but nothing beats it.

SWEETS, DESSERTS, CAKES

Stout Punch Ice Cream

For twelve

¾ cup plus 3 tbsp/ 220ml Guinness extra stout
2½ cups/600ml whole milk
2 x 3-inch/7.5cm cinnamon sticks
¼ tsp grated nutmeg
8 egg yolks
¾ cup/150g granulated sugar
2½ cups/600ml heavy cream, whipped to soft peaks
1 x 14-oz/397g can of condensed milk
Crushed peanut brittle (optional), to decorate

Pour the Guinness into a small saucepan and bring it to a boil on medium–high heat. Lower the heat to a rolling simmer and cook for 20–30 minutes, until it has reduced by roughly a third. Turn off the heat and set aside.

Pour the milk into a separate saucepan and place it on medium–low heat with the cinnamon and nutmeg. Once bubbles start to form at the edge of the milk, turn off the heat and let the hot milk infuse for 15–20 minutes.

In a medium mixing bowl, beat together the egg yolks and sugar. Discard the cinnamon sticks from the milk and slowly pour it into the egg mixture, stirring continuously, until fully incorporated. Rinse out the pan and pour the egg-and-milk mixture back into the same pan. Place the pan on medium–low heat and stir continuously with a wooden spoon until it thickens to a thin custard that coats the back of the spoon (5–10 minutes, be patient). Remove the pan from the heat and let the custard cool. Pour the cooled custard into a bowl and chill it for about 1 hour.

Combine the chilled custard and whipped cream in a bowl, and stir in the condensed milk. Add 1 tablespoon of the cooled Guinness syrup, taste and if you want it a little stronger add another small spoonful. Stir to combine, then transfer the mixture to a lidded plastic container and chill it overnight (this will help to create a super-smooth ice cream).

Once the mixture is chilled, strain it through a fine sieve and pour it into your ice-cream maker. Churn it according to the manufacturer's instructions until softly scoopable. Transfer the ice cream to a freezer-proof container, pop on the lid, and freeze until needed. Remove the ice cream 10–15 minutes before serving, to allow it to soften a little. Sprinkle with the crushed brittle, if using, to decorate.

I love a good pear. The earthy sweetness of this fruit sometimes comes with floral notes, at other times with hints of vanilla—and much else between. A good pear is simple and scrumptious, and poached and served with rum cream makes for an uncomplicated, almost effortless dessert. This is a very clean and refreshing end to any meal. (Perhaps now is the time to confess that I've been known to start a meal with dessert, too—because the simplest of indulgences, such as dessert before main, is sometimes everything we want or need.)

SWEETS, DESSERTS, CAKES

Poached Pears

WITH DARK RUM CREAM

For two

6 tbsp/75g granulated sugar, or more if needed
2-inch/5cm cinnamon stick, or more if needed
⅓ oz/10g ginger root, or more if needed, peeled and thinly sliced
2 ripe pears

For the rum cream
½ cup/120ml heavy cream
Dark rum, to taste
1 tsp powdered sugar, or to taste (optional)

Put 1 cup/240ml of water in a small saucepan with the sugar, cinnamon, and ginger. Check to make sure the pears will be submerged in the water; if not, double the quantities. Place the pan on medium–high heat and bring to a boil. Lower the heat and keep the liquid at a rolling simmer for 5 minutes to make sure the sugar has dissolved. Remove from the heat.

Peel the pears, cut them in half lengthwise, and core them (leave the stalks on if they are still intact). Transfer the pears to the pan with the sugar syrup and bring the liquid to a boil again. Lower the heat to a simmer, and poach the pears for 25–30 minutes, or until they are just tender. Let them cool slightly in the syrup.

Make the rum cream. In a large bowl, whip the cream until stiff peaks are just about to form. Beat in the rum to taste, then whip until you have stiff peaks, but making sure not to over-whip (I love butter, which is what over-whipping will end up with, but we want to stick to cream). Fold in the powdered sugar, adding more or less to taste, if you wish (despite my sweet tooth, I don't use it at all).

Serve the pears in bowls with a little syrup drizzled over the top and a generous helping of the cream on the side.

Mum wasn't passionate about food, or so she would say, but what she loved, she obsessed over, and she would have lost her mind over this sorbet. The few times we visited the Caribbean together, I relished how her face lit up as she spoke about the fruits of her youth. More often, I can see her seated at my nan's, eating guineps and chatting. She moved to London as an eight-year-old girl, yet her memories were so clear. As she talked, I watched her become that girl, enjoying the fruits I had never heard of, or hardly tasted, with the same excitement I felt as when I had a really good pear.

The flesh of the custard apple has an undeniably creamy texture and flavor—just like the custard of its name. Removing the flesh from the seeds can be fairly involved, so it's a nice task to do while you listen to something, making the job altogether more rhythmic and calming.

SWEETS, DESSERTS, CAKES

Custard Apple Sorbet

For four

Packed ½ cup/100g
   dark brown sugar
8 custard apples
2½ tbsp lime juice
   (about 1 lime), plus
   grated zest to
   decorate
2 tsp ground cinnamon
2 tsp ground ginger

Tip the sugar and 3 tablespoons of water into a small saucepan and place on low heat. As soon as the sugar has dissolved, take the pan off the heat and set the syrup aside.

Cut your custard apples in half, then scoop out the flesh into a medium bowl, discarding the seeds (it's really important to discard the seeds as they are toxic). Add the lime juice and both spices and, using an immersion blender, blitz the flesh to make a purée. Stir in ½ cup/120ml of your sugar syrup and let cool.

Once cool, churn the mixture in an ice-cream maker according to the manufacturer's instructions, until softly scoopable. Transfer the sorbet to a freezer-proof container, pop on the lid, and freeze for at least 10–15 minutes to firm up before serving. (You can freeze the sorbet longer—just remove it from the freezer to soften up a little before scooping into bowls.) If you don't have an ice-cream maker, spoon the mixture directly into a freezer-proof container and place it in the freezer for 2–3 hours, removing every 30 minutes or so to break up the ice crystals with a fork. It won't be quite as creamy, but it will be just as delicious.

Serve decorated with a little grated lime zest.

Rum, Rhum, Ron.

I think about all those times I've seen the people I love the most giddy with a punch or rum in hand: our annual Mitchell barbecue, where I could never make the rum punch quick enough; the neon pink hues of the liquid, in bowls with rum-soaked cut fruits; the sight of my grandad, and the men of his generation, wearing trilby hats and sharp suits at family functions, propping up walls with white plastic cups in hand; games of dominoes outside rum shops; the sound of melodic Caribbean accents and raucous laughter as night creeps in.

Joy is entwined with pain. Strength, resilience and hope are embodied in a drink. And so, I close this book with a chapter dedicated to rum, the bedrock of any Caribbean celebration, a spirit that represents the turbulent history of the islands, and is so much more than the sum of its parts.

I like my syrups strong and richly flavored. Depending on whether you prefer a thinner or thicker simple sugar syrup, you can choose to use either a weaker dilution of sugar to water or a stronger one (I vote the latter). I always use dark brown sugar, too; however, you can use light brown or, more usually, white for a softer touch.

RUM, RHUM, RON

Sugar Syrup

¾–1½ cups/150–300g granulated or dark brown sugar
1 cup/240ml water

Place the sugar and water in a small saucepan on medium heat, stirring occasionally until the sugar has dissolved. Take the pan off the heat and transfer the syrup to a sterilized jar or bottle. Store it in the fridge until needed. A weaker syrup will last around four weeks; stronger around six months.

Ginger Syrup

1¼ cups/250g granulated or dark brown sugar
½ cup/120 ml water
9 oz/250g ginger root, peeled and sliced

Place the sugar and water in a small saucepan on medium heat, stirring occasionally until the sugar has dissolved. Add the ginger and cook on a low simmer for 15 minutes to infuse the syrup. Take the pan off the heat and allow the syrup to cool with the ginger until it reaches your desired strength, testing it often. I like to steep mine for at least 1 hour. Strain the syrup into a sterilized jar or bottle, discarding the ginger slices. It should keep for one to two weeks in the fridge.

Sorrel Ginger Syrup

3½ oz/100g sorrel
4¼ oz/120g ginger root, peeled and chopped
1 cup plus 2 tbsp/220g granulated or dark brown sugar
3-inch/7.5cm cinnamon stick
4 pimento berries (optional)
3 cloves (optional)
Peel of 1–2 oranges (optional), to taste
1 quart/1 liter water

Get everything in a deep saucepan, including whichever spices you're using, and the water (which should just cover). Place the pan on medium–high heat and bring the liquid to a boil, stirring continuously to dissolve the sugar. Then, lower the heat to a simmer and cook the syrup for 15 minutes for the flavors to infuse. Turn off the heat, place the lid on the pan, and allow the syrup to steep overnight. Strain the infused syrup into a sterilized bottle. It will keep for one to two weeks in the fridge.

Sorrel, as hibiscus is known in the Caribbean, is a sure sign that Christmas is coming—a time when the fresh flowers are widely available (although you can now get dried sorrel year-round). The flowers are picked and dried, then boiled with spices to make a syrup, which is then mixed with rum and served over ice—our punch to others' nog.

I live in London, so as much as I love this infusion cold on a warm, sunny day, I also like serving it warm when it's cold and grey outside (far more usual in London than the snow-covered streets I dream of at Christmas). It's like a tropical hot toddy. Most of all, it's *very* drinkable, so you might want to do as I do and make a whole bottle. Keep it chilled in the fridge and serve just as it is, or reheat it and serve warm.

RUM, RHUM, RON

Sorrel Ginger Toddy

For two

¾ cup/180 ml Sorrel
  Ginger Syrup (page
  223)
3 tbsp dark rum
3 tbsp white rum
7 tbsp/100ml water
Ice cubes (optional),
  to serve
Slices of orange
  (optional)

Place all the ingredients in a pitcher and stir to mix. Put a few ice cubes into two tumbler glasses and pour the drink equally into each. Serve immediately.

Alternatively, for a hot toddy, place the ingredients in a small saucepan, with one or two orange slices, if you want to up the citrus, and heat on low heat until warm. Serve in heatproof glasses.

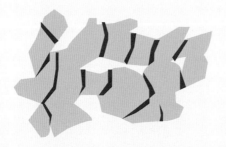

On his way back from ping-pong, my dad would grab a late-night snack from the Caribbean take-out restaurant, and with it a little styrofoam cup, wrapped in plastic wrap, for my mum. She would take it, have a sip, then likely place it in the fridge to enjoy the following day. In these moments she laid in me the foundations for the treat that is delayed gratification (along with the importance of finding pleasure in food). This punch was the only request Mum had when she was in the hospital, days before she died. In her final moments, she was still teaching me lessons about life: have the things you love, savor food, cherish our culture, and never stop being determined.

I've given quantities that work for me—feel free to have more of everything on hand, and adjust as necessary to make it work for you. Historically, I always found the punch too creamy, but its significance in my life meant it was impossible not to include it in the book. When I made it recently, it tasted different; I liked it. I guess Mum's still teaching me the joy of delayed gratification.

RUM, RHUM, RON

B's Pineapple Punch

For six

1 quart/1 liter fresh
  pineapple juice
7 tbsp/100ml
  condensed milk
1 tsp vanilla extract
½ tsp ground
  cinnamon
½ tsp grated nutmeg
½ tsp pumpkin pie
  spice
Whole milk or water,
  to taste
Ice cubes (optional),
  to serve

Add all your ingredients except the milk or water to a blender or food processor and mix to combine. Taste and adjust the flavors, adding a little more of any that need strengthening, according to your preference. Once you're happy, transfer the drink to a jar or pitcher to chill it before serving—it's best cold (alternatively, you can serve it straight away, but over ice).

Guinness or stout punch apparently has its origins in a sailor's drink by the name of Flip, a mixture of rum, ale, and molasses, served hot. Although I'm sure there is truth in this, I suspect the Irish immigrants that were in Jamaica around the same time also had something to do with it.

Versions vary from recipe to recipe, but I found that including almond milk results in a very smooth and dangerously drinkable concoction—the kind that loosens the limbs and relaxes the tongue. If you want to keep it vegan, swap out the condensed milk for coconut condensed milk instead.

RUM, RHUM, RON

Guinness Punch

For four

2¾ cups/650ml
  Guinness extra stout
1¼ cups/300ml almond
  or oat milk
1 x 14-oz/397g can of
  condensed milk
2 tsp vanilla extract
1 tsp ground cinnamon
½ tsp grated nutmeg,
  plus extra to serve
Splash of rum
  (optional), to taste
Ice cubes (optional),
  to serve

Place all the ingredients (except the ice) into a blender or food processor and pulse until combined. Thoroughly chill the mixture and serve without ice in a tall glass; or serve straight from the blender in a tall glass over ice. Sprinkle a generous grating of nutmeg on top to finish.

Orange and syrup was one of my favorite drinks as a child. On a hot day, nothing was able to quench my thirst like it. Usually, it came as an equal blend of orange or mixed-fruit cordial with either raspberry or strawberry syrup and water. That syrup was neon, and when I recently had some, I was buzzing for days. This punch pays homage to my childhood neon sugar-love and is a classic that you'll find at any Caribbean event. Where there are Caribbeans, there is rum punch, and for that I am thankful. I enjoyed my first taste of rum punch on my parents' tenth wedding anniversary. I was found passed out on top of my bed, in my bodysuit, after I had cheekily helped myself to some of the fruits that had been soaking in it all day. Not my finest hour, but it gave me a taste for the better things in life.

I make a rum punch by pouring things in until it tastes nice, but have always used a combination of white and dark rum and ginger wine. I can safely say it's my signature. Sadly, ginger wine is not available in North America, so I've offered an alternative. But if you ever find yourself on my side of the pond, sneak a bottle or two back for this punch. It's perfect in the height of summer, or when you need to bring a little summer energy through.

RUM, RHUM, RON

Summer Rum Punch

Yields about
7⅔ cups/1.8 liters

⅔ cup/160ml lime juice
(4–5 limes)
1 cup/240ml orange
juice
1 cup/240ml pineapple
juice
1 cup/240ml grenadine
½ cup/120ml dark rum
½ cup/120ml white rum
½ cup/120ml ginger
wine or ginger liqueur
(or ¼ cup/60ml sweet
marsala wine plus ¼
cup/60ml ginger
syrup)
2½ cups/600ml water

To serve
Ice cubes
Chopped fruits
Angostura bitters
Grated nutmeg

Combine the lime juice, orange juice, pineapple juice, grenadine, dark and white rums, and ginger wine in a pitcher. Stir in the water. Pour this into a sterilized bottle and store in the fridge until you're ready to serve—it will keep for two weeks and is anyway better after a few days or even a week.

For each serving, add a few ice cubes to a large tumbler, along with a few of your favorite chopped fruits, if you wish. Pour in the rum mixture to fill and add a couple of dashes of angostura bitters. Finish with a grating of nutmeg.

A friend gave me a little Caribbean cookbook and in it there's a rhyme that reads: "One for sour/two for sweet/three for strong, and/four for weak." Not only is it really good for thinking about making cocktails, but the rhyme softens me and makes me smile whenever I'm in need of decompressing, which can be often. It's for a planter's punch, a drink that is centuries old, and in its most basic form is simply rum, water, lime juice, and sugar syrup (as seen in my TT Lime on page 234). This recipe, then, I suppose, is my take on a planter's, using one of the most versatile flavors in the Caribbean. Tamarind has range. How you use it really depends on what you want it for and its ripeness. I've added it here for the sourness—I wanted the tang.

RUM, RHUM, RON

Tamarind Sparkler

For four

¼ cup/60ml tamarind juice or a block of tamarind paste to make a juice (see method)
½ cup/120ml Ginger Syrup (page 223)
¾ cup/180ml white rum
1 cup/240ml sparkling water
Lime wedges (optional), to serve

If you can't find tamarind juice, you can make it with a block of tamarind paste. Cut the block up and place it in a heatproof bowl. Pour in boiling water to just cover (this will create a thicker juice). Let the tamarind soak for 30 minutes, or until the paste has softened and you can separate the tough bits of pulp with your hands. Stir to dissolve the paste and then strain the liquid through a medium-mesh sieve into another bowl (don't use too fine a sieve, as the juice will be harder to push through). Make sure to scrape the tamarind that collects underneath the mesh. Pour the juice into sterilized ice-cube trays and freeze it in cubes. Now you have tamarind juice whenever you need it (defrost it first, if it's frozen; one cube is about 2 tablespoons, but check your tray).

To make the cocktail, place the tamarind juice, ginger syrup, white rum, and sparkling water in a blender or food processor and pulse in short bursts to combine. This gives the cocktail a little froth, which is nice when serving. Put a few ice cubes into each of four tall glasses and divide the cocktail between them. Finish with a squeeze of lime into each glass, if you wish (I prefer without).

Mum very rarely drank, but every now and then she'd have a Baileys or a snowball, usually at Christmas, or the occasional punch. When I was fourteen, though, and on vacation at Disneyland, Florida, she had a sip of my dad's frozen margarita—and then kept the whole drink as her own. She ended up so tipsy she shouted expletives at the entertainment and giggled from behind a menu as we tried to order food. Mum was a very funny drunk. Many years after that Floridian adventure, she became partial to Joe's Trini Lime punches at Island Social Club. Whenever she visited, she'd have a couple, then walk out smiling and swaying.

Joe keeps his recipe a closely guarded secret, so TT Lime (named for its Trinidad and Tobago roots) is instead a shoutout to his mixing mastery. And it also honors Ancil, my dad's Trinidadian best friend, who told me to use quick fermented lime, which adds a subtle funkiness that I love.

RUM, RHUM, RON

TT Lime

For six

1⅔ cups/400ml lime juice (about 10 limes)
2 cups/480ml water
Packed 2⅓ cups/500g dark brown sugar
2 x 3-inch/7.5cm cinnamon sticks
10 cloves
2 cups/480ml of your favorite rum
Angostura bitters, to taste
Ice cubes (optional), to serve

Place the lime juice in a sterilized jar and keep it at room temperature for at least 24 hours, or up to three days (this is your quick fermented lime).

Pour the water into a medium saucepan on medium heat. As soon as it starts to boil, take the pan off the heat and add your sugar, cinnamon sticks, and cloves. Stir to dissolve the sugar and then let the syrup cool and infuse. Add the lime juice and stir to mix. Finally, add the rum and a few dashes of angostura bitters, to taste.

You can allow the cocktail to steep like this, in the fridge, for a few days if you like, before serving (remove the whole spices once you're happy with the strength of the infusion). Serve it in lowball glasses, either neat or over ice. (Mum liked hers over ice.)

We dream.

The written word has such permanence, with a weight that seems stronger than oral traditions of sharing wisdom and stories. Writing this book has been hard. I say this not to complain, but to recognize that I overcame a challenge that, at many points along the way, I could not see myself conquering. So many of the recipes here come from people who overcame great obstacles. I wish to acknowledge this; I would not have been able to share this food with you if they hadn't fought for themselves, and for us.

Speaking for myself, I come from a mother who had sickle cell and lupus, and who walked in this world with grace and humility, even though her body didn't offer her the support she deserved. A brother who at sixteen had his body fail, and who spent his next thirteen years living as though tomorrow was never guaranteed—but still made one-, two-, five-year plans; who would sit in the library, then the office by day and the hospital by night, with most people unaware he was ill. A father who oiled, combed, and braided my hair after our light—my mum—was taken from us without warning in the middle of a pandemic, just days before I became a parent myself. He made sure to hold me in the ways he could manage, and he continues to do so. These are my people. I was and I am loved by them, and I will always love them in return.

This is a book about the food of the Caribbean—and yet, food is a moving constant, which evolves as time and people move forward. I recently attended a panel discussion—a discussion that touched upon authenticity and cultural appropriation—where the chef Andrew Wong pointed out that "today's innovation is tomorrow's authenticity." At the time, I felt frustrated. Honoring the history of a dish is important to me; so often dispersed communities receive little recognition for their food contributions when they serve them up themselves, and yet when that same food comes repackaged through a Western lens, it's suddenly vogue. Ultimately my frustration comes down to respect. But, even then, I can see the truth of the statement. Without the ingenuity and innovation of our ancestors, most of the dishes we know and love from the Caribbean wouldn't exist. However—I think it's important to note that sometimes things don't need changing, and that we should celebrate them for what they are, and exactly as they are.

When I started my supper club in 2016, Ali—my brother's long-term partner before his death, the sister I always wanted—asked me where I wanted to go with it. Without pause, and with absolute certainty, I said—I want to write a book. I've always been a dreamer. As a kid, I wrote stories with weekly chapters that my friends might have genuinely enjoyed—anyway, they loved me enough to pretend that they did. Writing has always brought me solace; I could write the stories that one day I hoped might come true. This is a book by a dreamer from South London, who, in her freedom to dream, was able to show how exceptional her ancestors were, and how much they contributed to the world we live in today.

Cook's Notes

Plant-based diets — A number of recipes in the book are naturally suitable for a plant-based diet; others can easily be made so. Unless the recipe gives a specific alternative, you can swap butter, condensed milk, heavy cream, and cream cheese for their vegan equivalents.

Checking for doneness — To check when my meat is cooked, I often pierce into the flesh with a sharp knife, hold the knife there for 10 seconds, then withdraw it and quickly check the temperature of the flat side of the blade against my wrist. If the meat is cooked, the blade will be hot, so a quick, light touch will do the trick to tell me what I need to know. For white meat, you can also check that the juices run clear. Alternatively, a probe cooking thermometer is useful if you're looking for precision or certainty. The internal temperatures you're looking for are:

Chicken: 167°F/75°C
Pork: 145–153°F/63–67°C (medium to well done)
Lamb: 126–160°F/52–71°C (rare to well done)
Frog legs: 145°F/63°C
Fish: 140°F/60°C

Deep-frying — When deep-frying, use either a deep-fat fryer or a heavy-bottomed saucepan, filling the pan half of the way up the sides (two-thirds at most), which should allow for the oil to bubble up without spilling. I prefer to use sunflower or canola oil when frying, but any neutral oil is ideal.

I use a probe cooking thermometer to check when the oil reaches the required temperature—usually 356°F/180°C (which is hot enough to ensure that the food fries rather than simply soaking up the oil), but occasionally higher, in which case the higher temperature will be noted in the recipe. Alternatively, the handle of a wooden spoon can work just as well. Hold the spoon by the scooping end and dip the handle vertically into the hot oil. When bubbles appear around the tip, your oil is ready.

Fry in small batches, so the temperature doesn't decrease too much during cooking, and always allow the oil to come back to temperature before frying the next batch. Drain each batch well.

Toasting spices — Tip your spices into a dry, nonstick frying pan and toast them over low heat until fragrant—this should only take 2–3 minutes. Remove them from the pan and let them cool completely, then either store as they are to crush as needed, or blitz and store them ground in an airtight container. They'll stay good for 6 months (you can use them after this time, but their flavor will have lessened).

Turmeric — I love turmeric, but it does stain, so be careful when using it—protect your work surfaces, hands, and clothing. The color will eventually fade on surfaces and skin, but your clothes might not be so lucky!

Freshly squeezed juice — Always use freshly squeezed lime, orange, or lemon juice. Your dishes will taste better for it.

Kitchen towels — If you're wrapping, patting, or covering food with a kitchen towel, use one made of non-shedding fabric to avoid fibers catching on your food.

Caribbean Ingredients

Ackee — A fruit native to West Africa, from the same family as the lychee, this is Jamaica's national fruit and features in its national dish, Ackee and Saltfish. A savory fruit, it is poisonous when unripe, but takes on the taste and texture of scrambled eggs when cooked.

Breadfruit — This potato-like fruit is savored throughout the Caribbean. Roasted, baked, fried, or boiled, it derives its name from having a bready texture when ripe and cooked.

Callaloo — Both a dish and, in parts of the Caribbean, the colloquial name for dasheen leaves, an indigenous form of amaranth that tastes like spinach.

Cassava — Can be bitter or sweet, depending on how much cyanide is contained within the root. Native to South America, this starchy root tuber is toxic when raw but has a nutty flavor when cooked. I love it steamed and then fried, or it can be boiled, then mashed, fried, roasted, or pounded to make flour.

Chow chow — Chocho, christophene, chayote; a gourd with many names. A mild-flavored fruit that's great nestled in curries and stews, absorbing all the flavors it's immersed in, though it can be eaten raw in salads and pickles too, adding a welcomed pickled crunch.

Custard apple — The leathery exterior houses the creamiest of flesh, with a texture much like custard. The flavor is similar to that of banana or pineapple, but with light floral notes.

Malanga — A small root vegetable, also known as coco yam. Much like cassava, it has an earthy nutty flavor when cooked, and equally cannot be eaten raw.

Pimento — In Caribbean cuisine, pimento refers to allspice, a dried unripe berry. Picked when green, it dries to dark brown with a hint of red and looks like a large peppercorn. A berry with notes of cinnamon, black pepper, star anise, fennel, nutmeg, and clove, it's a warm and versatile spice that can be used in both sweet and savory dishes.

Plantain — A gift from the heavens. You can eat plantain raw, but it's more often eaten cooked. Plantain is cooked at all stages of ripeness, from green to yellow to black. Plantain crisps and tostones call for green plantain, whereas straight fried plantain is cooked from just-ripened yellow to almost black.

Scotch bonnet — A mighty chile pepper with a sweet and fruity base flavor and a fiery heat that lingers on the tongue during and after eating. It can be found in all hues, from green to orange to red, and, though hot, can add incredible depth of flavor to dishes.

Sorrel — Native to the South Pacific and Asia, sorrel (as hibiscus is known in the Caribbean) is dried and then boiled with water, sugar and spices to make a drink traditionally consumed at Christmas. The earthy notes of these flowers also lend themselves to making savory dishes or dipping sauces.

Yam — A mildly sweet and earthy tuber that is both nutritious and versatile; its neutrality allows it to shine in many a recipe, all the while boosting brain health (apparently).

1 Ackee   7 Malanga

2 Breadfruit   8 Pimento

3 Callaloo   9 Plantain

4 Cassava   10 Scotch Bonnet

5 Chow Chow   11 Sorrel

6 Custard Apple   12 Yam

My Thanks

Wow—I am so incredibly grateful to have been able to create this work alongside and with the support of some very special people. I now understand when people say there are too many people to thank, for there are, and it is likely I will forget a few but I am deeply thankful to anyone and everyone who has been on this journey with me.

First, to my Particular Books family. Richard—thank you for seeing the vision I always thought was there but would let the outside voices tell me wasn't; for being excessively patient when my world fell apart, and for making my dream come true—working with you is a delight. To Sam, for the incredible editing and joy; to Amandeep and Millie for all the organizing, support, and excitement. Jude—your attention to detail knows no bounds (even if it sent me a little mad to start), you are a powerhouse—thank you.
To Emma, for taking my words and bringing them alive with your design, along with Matt. I honestly couldn't have imagined the book would be *this* beautiful—my gosh.

To my agent, Milly, who very swiftly became a friend. I can't put into words how appreciative I am of you. I remind myself daily you're the reason why sometimes you just need to trust your spidey senses. I have too many words, so I'm going to just thank you for everything; I could not have done it without you. To all at JULA, thank you for all you did to support us to get here, too. To Steven, thank you for your early work, that proposal was a looker!

To Lemara, Melek, Melissa, and Spasia—you have all subtly and not-so subtly held me physically, emotionally, and energetically for some, all or parts of this journey and I thank the angels for sending you to me when I needed you most. Watching you all thrive brings me unending joy—keep pushing boundaries, even when it feels like that ceiling is caving in. You're inspiring!

To Benji and Christian—wow, wow, wow. Look at the photos we made. The way we grew as a team during this process felt like family forming and energies blooming—a dream team. Thank you for letting me add the doilies and for allowing me to watch your talents—you're both very special beings. To Lily, Maria, and Zae, thank you for making sure the recipes worked and making the long days so much fun! Holly, Helen (and Dan and Marcie)—bless you for loaning your homes.

To the lads, lads, lads, drunk shirt crew and my faves—I love you all. Hannah, thank you for reading and editing my work, to always being there when I needed you. To Al, for looking after me like Mumma would have. To Eve, for making sure I could keep the lights on, for crying with me when my tears fell and for being the Sharkey to my George. To Dale, for making me feel seen, held, and heard. To Aoife, for absolutely everything (and Sam!). To Ivan, for cooking and holding baby M. To Anna, Luc, and Milla, for being our top buds. To Jon and Auntie O, for always checking in. To Thami and Dan, for saving the day. To Rachel, for always giving me space to write. To Janneke, Josh (sometimes you just have to miss the plane—ha), to Hanna, Jake, Madelene, Waylon, Harriet, Ali G, Clover, Emily & Emily, Nikki, Chloe, Pete, Just, Richi, Naus, Tamsin, Twembi, Claire, Sarah, Louise, and the Baresi family. Each of you made sure that I was here to write this today. Your messages, invitations, support, dinners, gifts, and presence honestly saved me—thank you.

To Frankie, Jen, Nim, Chiron, and Alena—the sisterhood of Black women is like no other thing in this world, and you're mine. I love you.

To the Blaineys—Amanda and Michael, you have always seen something in me and have been the most supportive mentors. I am immensely grateful to have you as chosen family, along with the most beautiful humans you created.

To my families—all of them. The Mitchells, Archers, Gloziers, Travers, ISC and Pop's Kitchen—thank you for the unwavering faith and for coming on this wild ride, it's been a journey! An extra shoutout to Auntie Dawn: I love you and you're so special. To Farrah—for making sure my mother's love is draped around my neck, always; and to Leisha for having relentless belief in me since the days of clogs and gingham two-pieces.

So, to my last thanks. Ali—thank you for being the sister I always wanted, for your kindness, humor, and incredible strength.

To Richie, the greatest, funniest, silliest, and most annoying brother in semi-equal measure. I miss you so much. I am always motivated by how you lived life, even when it was dangled in front of you so often. To Mumma, I heard you squeal with pride with each and every word I wrote. To have been mothered by you was an honor— I can only hope I am doing half the job you did. To hold you again will be the sweetest day. To Pops, I am so proud of you for still being here. It has been anything but easy, but we shall thrive together, and we will do it with joy in our hearts—thank you for your love and guidance, always. To Danny, the last few years have been brutal, but you never gave up on me, us, or this dream. You are my best friend, who catches me when I fall, even when I can't see you through the fog. Thank you, my love. And to our babe, Marcie, you saved me my darling. I love you to the moon and back.

Index

First published in 2024 by Particular Books, a part of the
Penguin Random House group of companies.

For information about permission to reproduce
selections from this book, write to Permissions,
W. W. Norton & Company, Inc.,
500 Fifth Avenue, New York, NY 10110

For information about special discounts for bulk purchases,
please contact W. W. Norton Special Sales at
specialsales@wwnorton.com or 800-233-4830

Manufacturing by Toppan Leefung
Designer and illustrator: Emma Hall
Photographer: Christian Cassiel
Project editor: Judy Barratt
Food stylist: Benjamina Ebuehi
Prop stylist: Tabitha Hawkins
Indexer: Ben Murphy
Production manager: Anna Oler

ISBN 978-1-324-08921-6

W. W. Norton & Company, Inc.
500 Fifth Avenue, New York, NY 10110
www.wwnorton.com

W. W. Norton & Company Ltd.
15 Carlisle Street, London W1D 3BS

1 2 3 4 5 6 7 8 9